Sensory Parenting
for Sensory Children

of related interest

**The Autism Discussion Page on Stress,
Anxiety, Shutdowns and Meltdowns**
**Proactive Strategies for Minimizing Sensory,
Social and Emotional Overload**
Bill Nason
ISBN 978 1 78592 804 8
eISBN 978 1 78450 834 0

Can I tell you about Sensory Processing Difficulties?
A guide for friends, family and professionals
Sue Allen
ISBN 978 1 84905 640 3
eISBN 978 1 78450 137 2

Understanding Sensory Processing Disorders in Children
A Guide for Parents and Professionals
Matt Mielnick
ISBN 978 1 78592 752 2
eISBN 978 1 78450 568 4

Sensory Parenting for Sensory Children

Tanya van Dalen

Illustrated by Ingrid Cutting

Jessica Kingsley Publishers
London and Philadelphia

First published in Great Britain in 2023 by Jessica Kingsley Publishers
An imprint of Hodder & Stoughton Ltd
An Hachette UK Company

1

A CIP catalogue record for this title is available from
the British Library and the Library of Congress

ISBN 978 1 83997 254 6
eISBN 978 1 83997 255 3

Printed and bound in Great Britain by TJ Books Limited

Jessica Kingsley Publishers' policy is to use papers that are natural,
renewable and recyclable products and made from wood grown in
sustainable forests. The logging and manufacturing processes are expected
to conform to the environmental regulations of the country of origin.

Jessica Kingsley Publishers
Carmelite House
50 Victoria Embankment
London EC4Y 0DZ

www.jkp.com

MIX
Paper from
responsible sources
FSC® C013056

Contents

Part 3: Sensory Strategies and Making a Plan

Acknowledgements

I would like to thank Professor Janet Treasure for giving me permission to apply the animal analogies to sensory children and rewrite them for this book.

This book was born and developed within a community of incredible people. Noni and Peter Farrelly (founders of Grow-baby International) believed in me when I didn't, supporting me every step of the way. Ingrid gave me hours of her time creating stunning images from my jumbled thoughts. Raelene set deadlines to keep me on track and read through terrible versions of chapters. Her prayers kept me going. Kirby became my test ground for the content and was always honest and encouraging. My church family prayed and loved my family through the best and the worst of days. My incredible friends, you know who you are, believed in me and cheered me on. You are the best ones anybody could ask for.

My colourful, neurodiverse family who said 'yes' without hesitation to sharing some of our story. Lyska and Saskia, I am so proud to be your mother. Morné, my misunderstood rhino, I love being your wife.

Papa, you have always been there for us, believing the best even at our worst.

My God in heaven, thank you.

This book is dedicated to my mother. She never met any of her grandchildren but her desire to love my brother, sister and

I more than she ever was built deep foundations of love in us. She would be proud of our families.

Introduction

I sit with a mother who is close to tears. She tells me that she has read every book and online blog she can find about 'how to parent'. She has marble jars on the kitchen counter and sticker charts on the fridge to help encourage her child to 'behave'. She has spent too much money on Lego as a reward, yet nothing seems to help. What almost hurts more than her own perception of failing as a parent is her family who tell her she should be stricter and stop pandering to her child. She feels confused and upset because the techniques that work for all her other friends just don't work for her child. And she is tired. Tired of feeling as if it is all her fault. This is the harsh reality for many of us who have parented a child with sensory processing difficulties.

A sensory processing disorder (SPD) occurs when our brain struggles to process and integrate the information that it receives coming in from the senses (we will look at this in more detail in Chapter 1). Sensory processing difficulties are most often found alongside another diagnosis, for example autism, attention deficit hyperactivity disorder (ADHD), obsessive compulsive disorder (OCD), avoidant restrictive food intake disorder (ARFID), anxiety, genetic disorders or other learning disabilities. SPD can also occur without another diagnosis so it is important to get professional help when putting together the puzzle for your child or even for yourself. Sometimes sensory processing difficulties can 'look' like autism or ADHD and an experienced professional can help you find out which it might be.

Parenting a child with sensory needs is upside down and back to front. Sometimes the approaches that work for other children, even siblings, just don't work for our children. 'Top-down' approaches that require our child to behave in a certain way to avoid a consequence or earn a reward can set our children up to fail. Top-down approaches rely on the child to think through the reward or punishment that is related to their behaviour and choose to change what they say or do. Our kids often just don't have a choice about whether they can conform to what a particular moment requires. Their bodies simply react without time to think it all through.

There are as many ways to parent as there are parents and children on the earth. Your DNA is unique, your experience of being raised is your own and not one other human in the world like you has ever existed or ever will. The same is true for your child; there is not one other human like them and your relationship with each other is completely your own. It is therefore logical that no book or professional could ever give advice that completely works for your family or for you every time. As Winnie Dunn explains, any behaviour we see can have multiple explanations as to the meaning or purpose because humans, and the way we behave, are complex (Dunn 2008). This book is not a recipe for you to follow to fix all that is not working or, worse still, another thing added to your to-do list to make you feel guilty. It is meant to help you take a moment to think slightly differently about how you parent your child and find the moments when you are already doing well.

We will start this journey by taking time to understand what is happening for our sensory children, especially focusing on when they become overloaded and go into meltdown. However, this is not only a journey about your child. You will learn more about the way your own body and brain react. A deeper understanding of your sensory child can change how you parent. More than this, science tells us that being emotionally connected to a human who understands what we need changes the way our nervous system functions.

Let's start with social baseline theory, as it gives us the first small piece of the puzzle. Dr James Coan, a neuroscientist and clinical psychologist at the University of Virginia, set about trying to prove the theory that when life gets tricky, we feel safer and more secure when we surround ourselves with others we have a connection with (Coan & Sbarra 2015). He conducted an experiment using electrodes to administer pain to a group of people. What he found was fascinating. The person being hurt felt significantly less pain when they had someone whom they trusted and were emotionally connected to alongside them. Having a stranger sitting with them had very little effect on the pain the subjects felt. What Dr Coan proved is something we all probably know instinctively. Our bodies and brains become physically calmer in the presence of a person who really knows who we are, someone we feel is on our side (Rheem 2018). It makes sense if we think about it, that we function best around someone who understands us and knows what we need without being told. That colleague who quietly places a cup of tea on your desk after a tricky meeting, the friend who sees you are stressed as soon as you walk into the coffee shop, or your mother who knows just what to do to help you feel better.

This is exactly why everything changes when we gain more knowledge about what our children are experiencing. Knowing how powerful our presence is to others will help shape how we communicate with them. We may not have a magic wand that can instantly take our children out of their distress but simply knowing more about what is happening in their body and brain can equip us to react differently. There will be times when we cannot change the way our children process sensory input and no matter what we do, we can't prevent a meltdown. There is, however, something we can change. We can change how *we* react and in doing so, we can change how our child experiences the moment. The subjects being shocked were still exposed to the same level of pain but the way they *perceived* the pain changed when they were not alone. This is the power we hold as parents and carers; we can change the background soundtrack that is playing when our child becomes distressed. We can be the safe and stable place where they can learn to regulate their strong emotions. And in time we will learn how to help them regulate as best as they can with the tools they have.

We must not be tempted to look at how our children behave only on the surface and label it one way or another. Behaviour is hardly ever just what it seems to be on the surface; it is rarely just one thing. We need to embrace the idea that our children are complex and that there are many layers to their reactions to the world.

We are going to look at one layer, one aspect. We will take time to understand what sensory processing is, what happens when we fall out of our window of tolerance and move into fight, flight and freeze mode – and, most importantly, how our responses are as important as the sensory tools we implement. This book is not the answer to all the questions we may have, but it might be a good place to start. After all, as we will discover, we are a powerful tool and are best placed to help our children learn to navigate this planet and become the best version of themselves they can be.

★ *Part 1* ★

UNDERSTANDING OUR SENSORY EXPERIENCES

Chapter 1

What Is Sensory Processing?

We are all sensory beings. From inside the womb until we take our final breath, every human relies on their sensory system to survive, to have fun, to relax, to love, to learn, to work. Learning about the sensory system is best done through your own experience of how your body takes in and processes information from your eight senses. Yes, eight!

You may be tempted to read the next chapters with only your child in mind. I want to invite you to think of your own sensory systems as we travel through the next chapters together. Think about what you experience every day and what your body needs to feel calm and grounded as well as what your child is experiencing.

A deeper understanding of both your own and your child's sensory needs will develop your compassion. Knowing that some of the behaviours you see in your child, the ones that can appear to make their own lives more difficult at times, are not a choice they are making but rather the way they have been created might give you insight into their lives. When we have a deeper understanding and empathy, we will totally change the way we react. Perhaps you may even find some of yourself in here too.

This is the beginning of your journey to being more in control and more chilled out!

30 seconds to experience it

Think of your morning routine. Do you like to be woken with the radio and music playing? Or do you need it to be quiet? Hot cup of coffee or a glass of cold juice? Warm shower or soak in the bath? Are you someone who feels ready for the day after a run or a visit to the gym? Does the thought of running before the day even starts make you feel ill? Do you enjoy the noise of children playing first thing in the morning or do you wake up 15 minutes early so that you have a little bit of quiet time before they wake?

The background music to our lives is sensory. If you love a warm milky drink to start the day, you will feel a bit off-centre if you can only have sour grapefruit juice. If you love a quiet, slow start to the day, you may be overwhelmed if you have to put on running shoes and jog. Equally, if your body needs the heavy muscle work and movement of a run, you may feel off-balance all day if you have missed going.

Our sensory system underlies all of who we are and every human in the world uses it to find ways to feel safe and connected to others.

An introduction to sensory processing

It is Christmas Eve, you have to go to the supermarket, and you have to take your toddler. Tomorrow your mother-in-law is coming to lunch and you have a list of impossible ingredients to find. What *is* star anise anyway? The last time you bought spices it was also Christmas; now they are out of date and you have to buy them again. When you arrive, it takes you ages to find a place to park, and it is raining hard outside and freezing cold. Your toddler is not happy about this trip and is letting you know. You aren't happy about this trip either, but you don't have the luxury of screaming about it. Being little has its perks.

The way your body processes sensory input is going to make this task unpleasant but manageable. Or the way your body processes sensory input will awake the crazy, loose-cannoned person you know lives inside you – the one you work hard to hide away, especially in public!

Good sensory processing means you get out of your car and you are able to tolerate the wet clothes as you get soaked through. You can ignore the hot air that blasts you as you walk through the front door of the supermarket. If your sensory processing is working well, you hear Wham! sing about their 'Last Christmas' and you can tune it out, fighting the urge to smash the sound system into tiny pieces. You can keep your eye on the toddler as she trots next to you because she wouldn't sit in the trolley. And you are able to do this all the way around the supermarket without losing her. You can navigate your trolley around all the other stressed-out shoppers without knocking down the lady who for some reason is in every aisle you turn into even though she is crawling at slow speed. Then you remember you are also slow because the toddler is stopping to look at every crack in the floor! Good sensory processing means you can ignore all the people brushing past you, touching you as they squeeze past. You are able to keep focused, find the spices aisle, scan the contents and single out star anise. In the bottle, you notice that it looks like a flower, quite pretty actually.

Good sensory processing enables you to make it around the aisles, collect everything on the list and make it back to the car with all the shopping and, critically, the toddler. Good sensory processing means you didn't lose the plot with the slow lady when she stopped suddenly in front of you, you didn't sarcastically snarl at her under your breath as you swerved around her, narrowly missing her ankle with your trolley. No, you kept your cool.

You can see how the entire trip could be different if you found one of those senses difficult to process. If the wet clothes were intolerable, if the hot air disorientated you, if you could not navigate the aisles and people with the trolley or if scanning all the spice labels to find the right one was impossible. But, more importantly, if all of these sensory experiences made your brain go into a state of fight or flight, then you may well have lost the toddler at some point or the police would be called due to your shouting.

How our bodies process sensory input is unique to each of us. Every human ever born has used their senses to learn, survive and love in the world around them from inside the uterus until they no longer take a breath. Sensory processing is how we know if our bodies feel playful, calm, aroused or irritated, afraid or repulsed. The sensations not only from the outside world but also from inside our body are used as clues, alongside memories and knowledge to help us to know if we should run into the arms of a person or run as quickly as we can in the other direction. The way you process sensory information determines if you squeal with excitement as you are strapped into a rollercoaster or you offer to hold all the bags while your friends take the ride. Your unique sensory processing influences how you learn in a classroom or how you manage a busy conference centre.

So, what exactly is sensory processing? We will do a quick overview of a complex subject. There are some excellent books that can give you much more detail if you need it. See the end of the book for more resource suggestions. I have included some suggestions throughout this book.

What is sensory processing?

We all know the five senses that we are taught in primary school. These are touch, smell, taste, sight and hearing. When we look at sensory processing, we learn that there are three more senses, namely interoception (internal body messages), proprioception (body sense) and the vestibular sense (movement sense). We'll look at these three 'new' senses in more detail throughout this chapter, but first it's worth clarifying that sensory processing is simply how your brain takes all the information from these eight senses, deciphers it and tells you how to react. In the supermarket, your brain is working hard to ignore parts of your senses. You ignore the sound of Wham! but keep your ears open for the sound of your child's voice. You barely notice the unexpected touch of a person pushing past you so that you can use your proprioception (body sense) to navigate the trolley without knocking over the slow lady. Your brain instinctively focuses on some of your senses while ignoring others.

Interoception

30 seconds to experience it

Read these instructions fully and then find a place to sit comfortably and close your eyes.

Take a deep breath and focus in on your body. Notice how your body feels at this moment. Do you have a full bladder, do you have any aches or pains, are you hot or cold, hungry or thirsty? Do you have a knot in your stomach, do you feel stressed or peaceful?

What you have just experienced is interoception, messages your brain receives about what is going on inside your body. When we stop and listen to our bodies, we sometimes realise that we are hungry or thirsty but have not noticed, we are colder than we thought or, goodness, we need to run to the loo right now!

Interoception is the ability to read the signals from our body telling us what we need in a specific moment to survive. Do we need to warm our body up or cool it down? Do we need to drink fluids or eat in order to fuel ourselves? Is our bladder full or do we need to do a poo? We know that many of our sensory children find listening to their bodies tricky.

For example, a child who just does not register that they are getting hot. The day could be sweltering, they have been running around the park for an hour and they are beetroot red in the face. Yet, when you ask them, 'Are you hot? Shall we take that jumper off?' they simply look at you with a confused expression. 'Hot? No, I am fine,' they say as they run off into the shimmering heat of the playground. And you stand in the shade, perplexed as to why they just can't feel the heat!

It is not just our sensory kids who find it tricky to read signals from our body. As parents, we can find it hard too. How often have you made it to the end of the working day and as you get into your car thought, 'Gosh, I am hungry! When did I last eat?' Or you have been crazily running after the children all day and when you stop, you realise you have a headache from not drinking enough fluids. Or you flop into bed at night and only then realise you have a sore throat or possibly a temperature. When we are in a heightened state of emotion or are stressed or busy, our own interoception can be poor.

It is fascinating how interoception is intricately linked to emotion. Think about getting ready for a wedding. You choose your outfit, you wrap the gift, you slip on the shoes and check your hair in the mirror. Now you might wonder, what is this feeling in the pit of my stomach? Is it excitement about seeing all of your friends dressed up and ready to celebrate together? Are you nervous or anxious because you are a plus one and you have never met the bride or groom and so you worry you have a never-ending evening of small talk ahead of you? Are you coming down with the sickness bug doing the rounds at school? Or are you hungry as you overslept and missed the free breakfast buffet? You feel something in your body and then work out what this sensation means. It is a skill we need to learn to first note what our body is feeling and then link it to an emotion.

When we struggle with our interoception, we find it hard to know what we are feeling. We might find it more difficult to regulate our bodily functions.

Understanding this might explain why approaches such as mindfulness are so powerful. Learning to slow down and take note of your body is a great place to start to learn about what you need in that moment.

It can be a long process to help teach and build a sensory child's interoception. A brilliant place to start is the book by Cara Koscinski (2018), *Interoception: How I Feel*. Cara gives us some brilliant games to play to help nurture and grow interoception. In the meantime, it may help us understand why some of our children continue to soil themselves, especially when they have other things to focus on such as school or playing, why they can't tell us what they are feeling or name their emotions when we ask or why they don't notice they are getting overwhelmed until they are in full meltdown.

→ **Try this**

Next time your child or you begin to become overwhelmed, ask them to close their eyes and scan their body. You do the same. Ask some questions. What do you notice? Is your body trying to give you a message? Is your tummy saying feed me, your mouth saying I am dry? Are your muscles asking for you to use them to help you feel better? Help them become aware of the signals that interoception is sending them. It might help you too!

Understanding is the beginning of compassion, and that is sometimes the best place to start!

Proprioception (body sense)

30 seconds to experience it
Read all the instructions first before starting.

Put this book down and close your eyes. Stretch out your left arm in front of your face and hold one finger up. Now, with your right forefinger, touch the finger you are holding out, then your nose, and repeat a few times.

First, how easy was it for you to follow these instructions? Could you put the book down and instinctively do it? Did you have to do it bit by bit, for example first working out which is your left hand, then holding it out but then having to read the instructions again for the next bit? Did you keep your eyes open to make sure your arm was in the right position, in front of your face? And when you went to touch your finger and then your nose, did you find them first time with your eyes closed or did your right finger float around a little until it touched your left one?

What you just experienced was your proprioceptive system. This is the information that gets sent from your muscles and joints about where you are in space, how your body parts are placed in relation to each other and where you are in relation to objects or people around you. I asked you to close your eyes so that you could not employ your vision to give your brain information about where your left finger was. This meant you had to 'feel' where it was placed.

Proprioception or your body sense is the sense you use to go down the stairs in the dark when you need a snack in the middle of the night. If it is working well, you don't need to put on the light and alert the rest of the family; you instinctively know where to put your feet so that you don't fall down the stairs and wake them. Poor proprioception would require you to see where you need to place your feet, or to slow down and place each foot down carefully before continuing.

Our body sense also tells us how much force to use (see

30 seconds to experience it). When we pick up an egg in the kitchen or a rock in the garden, we instinctively know to use less force for the egg. But if our proprioceptive system is immature or not giving our brain the right information, we might use too little or too much force. We might be the child in the playground who knocks other children over all the time while playing because we can't really control how much force we use. Or you might be the parent who is continually saying, 'Don't slam the car door', or 'Be gentler when you put that glass down on the kitchen counter.'

Back to our trip to the supermarket on Christmas Eve. If your proprioceptive system is not working well, then you will find navigating the trolley around all the decorative piles of chocolate tins and the slow old lady tricky. You may need to use all your brain power to stop your trolley hitting the champagne display and because of that, you might inadvertently lose your toddler or forget what you were about to tick off the list!

Our proprioceptive system is the basis for learning gross and fine motor skills. If we have to think about how to move and place ourselves or how much force to use, it can be frustrating or exhausting. Catching a ball, riding a bike, learning to swim, doing ballet all need us to know how to move to get the outcome expected. Think of a child in the first year of school. Often large parts of the time they are taught on the floor in front of the teacher. The child with body sense difficulties will be the one that literally walks across the other children like Godzilla, knocking them over and sending reading glasses flying from faces. They aren't being unkind or thoughtless, they aren't being naughty. They simply can't get their bodies to navigate all the children in their way.

→ Try this

Try 'backwards chaining' when teaching a new skill to a child. This means you teach them the last step first, which gives them a sense of accomplishment, and then you slowly add other steps in one by one. For example, when making a sandwich, they put the second slice on top of an already made sandwich and cut it in half and then enjoy it! Next time they put the cheese on, then the slice and then cut it up. Then you put the mayonnaise onto the bread, they spread it, put the cheese on, then do the slice and cut. This gives them time, repetition and a sense of accomplishment. This simple principle can be used for any life skill such as dressing or tidying a room.

Understanding that for some of our sensory kids, learning new skills takes so much more mental effort or that they are not purposefully slamming the door, that they actually can't use less force when playing with their friends or throw the ball softly, is all part of us starting to view their behaviour through a new set of lenses. It really does change how we react if a child knocks the drink over when we know it is out of their control and not because they don't care about who cleans it up. We will have more patience teaching a child how to ride a bike or later drive a car if we know they need more time and the chance to practise in order to learn.

When we change how we react, they change how they feel about themselves.

30 seconds to experience it

Place a piece of paper on a soft surface like your duvet or a soft pile rug. Using a sharpened pencil or ball point pen, draw a picture of yourself.

Does the pencil pierce the paper easily? Do you have to use energy making sure you use the right amount of pressure in order not to pierce the paper? Does this make drawing the picture almost the second thing you can focus on?

This is another example of how your proprioceptive system can influence your confidence. Imagine you have to concentrate on how much pressure you use to write or throw a ball, you have to think about how to put a glass down on the table or how to close the car door. It would be exhausting and sometimes you would simply just not want to do it at all!

Vestibular (movement sense)

30 seconds to experience it
Read the instructions fully first before starting.

Stand up and lift one leg to balance on one foot. Do not hold on to anything to help you. Now, once you have gained your balance, close your eyes.

What you have just experienced is the vestibular system. Was it easy to balance with your eyes open? Did you notice yourself fixing your eyes on something in front of you to help hold your balance? When you closed your eyes, did you instantly lose your balance?

Tucked deep into your inner ear is a system that sends information to your brain about what your body position is in relation to gravity. It tells you if you are upside down, spinning or upright. This information is powerful and is related to so many parts of our lives.

Our vestibular system is the very first sensory system to develop in the womb and the one we use to soothe a baby. We use movement to calm a baby by rocking them back and forth or bouncing them on our knee. The vestibular system is powerful! The information sent from our inner ear can have a profound effect on us. It feeds into the part of our brain linked to muscle tone and eye movements, as well as attention and focus.

The vestibular system regulates your body's overall muscle tone which is needed to help keep us upright and stable. Sometimes, when our muscle tone is low, we are less stable in our pelvis or shoulder girdle or even our core. This can mean that we struggle to sit upright for long, and wriggle in our chair or rock back and forth. Our fine motor development may be delayed, or we might not be able to hold our body in positions for long.

The vestibular system is also linked to your eyes. Think of sitting on a stationary train and the train next to you moves. Have you ever felt as if you are moving too, even when you are not? That is your visual system stimulating your vestibular system. Our vestibular system helps us track our eyes across our field of vision and we need this to copy from the board or to scan the cereal boxes in the supermarket to find the one our mother-in-law eats.

Our brains can either need more movement than others or less.

When our child is under-responsive to vestibular input (movement) it may mean that they are continually on the move, looking for movement to stimulate their brain. They are the child who is always on the move. The need to move is out of their control; telling a child with an under-responsive movement system to 'sit still' is pointless. They would if they could.

If their muscle tone is low, then sitting upright in a chair or on the floor can also be near impossible. Moving about activates their muscles, helping them to maintain their posture. The product is a child who appears never to be still.

→ Try this

Instead of asking your movement-seeking child to sit still until everyone has finished eating dinner, give them the job of taking plates back to the kitchen counter while the others finish. If they get fidgety, ask them to get the ketchup from the fridge, the one you purposefully left there for that very reason. Teach them what their body needs while you are learning what that is too! Set them up to succeed.

Now let's refresh our knowledge of the senses more commonly known to us.

Tactile system (touch sense)

30 seconds to experience it

Take an old glove or sock, preferably one you can throw into the recycling afterwards. Fill it with a tablespoon of cornflakes (or any crunchy cereal) and then lightly crush them. Now put your foot or hand into the glove or sock.

What does it feel like? Do you like the sensation? Did you rip it off straightaway and then call someone else over to try it too, while you grimaced? Or are you the rare human who thought, this feels rather lovely; in fact I might add bran flakes to my gloves from now on?

Our sense of touch is powerful and one of the biggest factors in our ability to feel grounded and regulated. Some of us can hardly stand the feel of certain textures against our skin; we are ready to rip those work clothes from our bodies the moment we walk in through the door and put on a pair of soft, loose PJs. Wearing a pair of skinny jeans is torture as we can't stop feeling them press in on our skin; that tie we must wear to school makes us unable to breathe.

And our tactile system is vital in nurturing babies. My daughter hated me bathing her when she was a baby; she screamed the house down with every bath. But for her daddy, she smiled and cooed. I would get upset and my husband helpfully would say that I was just being too rough with her and needed to use lighter touch. The irony was that the lighter I made my touch, the more painful it was because her tactile system was so sensitive. She enjoyed him bathing her because he used firm, even pressure that she could tolerate more than the light touch. It remains that way for her now, aged 21. She does not like uninvited or unexpected touch and can easily go into a state of fight or flight when surrounded by too many people.

If you are over-responsive to touch, then you might hate standing in a queue at school and insist on being at the front so you can control how many people can touch you. You might feel as if someone has punched you when they simply brushed past you. You may hate certain clothing and insist on wearing the same outfits over and over. Brushing your teeth or washing your hair may feel like torture.

An over-responsive tactile system can cause many difficulties for us and send us into meltdown almost instantly.

We might also use our sense of touch to give us information

about the world and so touch everything, all the time. We may need to fidget while sitting, we might run our hands along the wall when walking home from school or we might not be trusted in the glassware section of the store as we want to pick everything up to have a feel.

And we can be both! We can struggle to tolerate touch and seek it out all the time.

➜ Try this

Imagine that a spider – a big hairy one – walks over your arm. Do you feel as if you want to rub that spot out of your skin? Did you know that the messages for light touch – the spider – get to your brain slower than the deep touch, your rubbing? Deep pressure overrides light touch so try using massage, roll your child tightly in a towel after a bath, encourage them to lie under heavy sofa cushions to do their homework or squash them under a therapy ball. Deep pressure is a great way of calming down an overwhelmed tactile system.

Auditory system (hearing sense)

30 seconds to experience it

Choose a cheesy song that you are not very fond of, maybe a nursery rhyme or that 1980s song you can't get out of your head once you have heard it. Get a pen and paper ready so that you can make a list of one word beginning with every letter of the alphabet starting from Z, X, Y and so on. Now, play the song loudly and start your list. Go!

Are you the person who could write that list with ease (amazing!) or did you need to stop and think harder about what to write? Did you accidentally write down one of the lyrics instead of the item on your list? Did you stop after a few seconds and turn the annoying song off? Or were you the person who used your voice to drown out the song by either speaking the list as you wrote it or yelling 'This is ridiculous' as you shut the activity down?

> Or did you find yourself zoning out, staring into the distance for a
> few seconds as you tried to get yourself back on task?

This is what it can feel like when you struggle with processing
auditory information. The information about sound coming
to your brain can be disrupted or distorted, causing you to be
overwhelmed and distracted. Often, we try to be louder than
the noise around us because we can control our own voices.

If you struggle with your auditory system on your trip around
the supermarket then you might not be able to ignore the
Christmas songs playing; in fact they will distract you enough
to make it tricky to follow your train of thought. When the
music suddenly stops so an announcement can be made, the
unexpected, loud sound can overwhelm you, making your heart
race and head spin. When you can't find the spice aisle, the
directions the staff member gives you will make little sense and
you will walk away wondering where to go.

Auditory processing difficulties can mean that you sometimes take longer to process the spoken information given to
you. This can make life more difficult, for example in school.
Here the teacher never gives just one instruction at a time so

that by the time you have worked out the first bit of what they said, they are already three steps ahead.

Think about getting your child ready for school. You give instructions like this, 'Where is your book bag? Don't forget to put your water bottle in like yesterday. I have filled it up for you and left it in the kitchen. Also, do you have PE today?' When you turn around and look again your child is playing Lego in the other room because they simply couldn't process all the instructions you gave.

We aren't talking about a child who has difficulty hearing – you have had their ears tested and they can hear fine!

And lastly, a child who finds noise overwhelming is not always the quiet one. Often, they are loud, very loud, to drown out the noise around them with their own voice. They are in control of their own voice after all.

→ Try this

When you give instructions, slow down. Make sure you have your child's attention first. Give them the instruction and ask them to repeat it back to you if needed. Wait until this is done then give the next. Leave enough time for this! For example, 'Go and get your book bag. Now go and get the water in the kitchen.'

Visual system

30 seconds to experience it

You need a pen and paper and a mirror. If you have a colouring page or a maze that would work well too. Place the paper at the base of the mirror and begin the maze, colouring or simply drawing a picture of your choice. The challenge is not to watch what you are doing on the paper but to watch what you are doing in the mirror.

How easy is it for you to work out which way to move the pen? Can you easily draw the picture or does the reversal confuse you?

The visual system has become our primary way of learning in the world; without sight, we need a large number of adaptations. However, it is the one sense often overlooked when a child is struggling in school. The visual system is complex and we do not have enough time to go into detail here. Let us think back to our trip around the supermarket to give us a flavour of how our visual sense may be impacted.

If you walk into the supermarket and you are immediately overwhelmed or distracted by the strip lighting in the ceiling or the busy, unpredictable way the people are moving, it could feed into your overload of the situation. Being over-responsive to visual input can cause a child to feel distressed and unsafe.

If you are not bothered by the busy supermarket or the occasional flickering light, you might have another difficulty and that might be using your vision to navigate the trolley around the aisles and people. Remember how our vestibular system (movement sense) is linked to vision? Our visual-motor skills are used to plan and execute movement, for example to know how to navigate our bicycle around a person in the way or to work out how much space there is in the aisle to push the trolley through. We need all our systems to work well together so we can smoothly scan the shelf for our cereal or glance up and check on the toddler and then look back down to the shopping list.

When our visual system is not working as it should, it can make school-based activities tiring and stressful.

★ *Chapter 2* ★

What Does Your Brain Do With All the Sensory Information?

Now we know what the eight senses are, let us have a look at what our brain does with this sensory information. Why do some of us become so quickly overwhelmed by our sensory systems?

Your daughter comes out of school with a birthday party invite waving in her hand. It is all glitter and rainbows, a unicorn princess party. She is grinning from ear to ear and telling you exactly what she wants to wear. A pink and purple party dress with sequins and frills. A crown with jewels, not plastic ones, real ones! And she must have a wand with glitter ribbons and shoes that go clippy-cloppy when she walks.

Your heart sinks and you feel a knot build in your stomach. Is it wine o'clock yet? A glance at your watch tells you that if you have wine now it will be a very bad thing, so you resist.

The reason your heart sinks is not because it will take hours scouring the internet to find the exact crown and shoes she wants. No, it is your experience of parties like this that causes the anxiety. Starting with the outfit. Even if you find the perfect one which she will be desperate to wear, it will be scratchy, and she will end up wearing her leggings and smiley face T-shirt. The same ones she wears all the time. This will make her feel sad before the party even starts because although she can't seem to wear the princess outfit for more than five minutes, she desperately wants to.

The party itself is already unfolding in your mind. Knowing the mother of the child, there will be an entertainer dressed as Sleeping Beauty or The Little Mermaid. They usually have a boom box and a microphone through which they will sing songs and yell instructions for dance moves. The kids will all consume sugar and become slightly unhinged and feral within about 24 minutes of arrival. The noise levels will rise, and there will be one or two kids who will relish in stomping on the balloons to pop them. The adults will drink their wine faster than needed on a Saturday afternoon. Now, you don't mind either way about how much wine they drink, but it means they get louder and take less notice of what their kids are up to.

And all this lovely, glittery mess will send your child spiralling at about 26 minutes in. She will feel sad about not wearing her carefully planned outfit. Plus, the noise will be too much, and she will struggle to follow the dance instructions yelled out by The Little Mermaid. A sensory meltdown is inevitable, and you won't get to talk to Jenny or Janet or Jimmy while sipping a cold glass of Chardonnay. No, you will be tucking a screaming, flailing child under your arm, trying to sneak out of the back door.

That is why your heart sinks when you see the invite in her little hands after school.

Ironically, your daughter is often the loudest one in the house or at a party and may be the one stomping on the balloons herself. She is always on the move, jumping about or hanging upside down on the sofa. She is not predictable; sometimes she loves a party and gets sad about leaving. It just doesn't always make sense and it is hard to predict.

30 seconds to experience it

How does your sensory system manage a loud, balloon-exploding children's party? Do you relish the idea of meeting new people and does the laughter and joy of a party fill you with excitement? Does your heart rate go up a little as you get anxious about the noise and chaos? Are you thinking of ways to get more involved at the party so you can stay longer or are you plotting a way to avoid it altogether?

It is just as important to take note of how your sensory system processes an environment. Yes, your child may struggle but what does that mean for you? Are you disappointed to have to leave early or anxious about it all before you even arrive? Keep thinking of your own needs as we continue our journey.

What might be going on? Sensory information from the eight systems we have discussed gets detected, integrated and modulated by the body and brain. This is a complex process but Carol Kranowitz (2005) has simplified it for us in *The Out-of-Sync Child* and I summarise that here.

Detection

Sensory input enters the brain through the peripheral nervous system. Imagine a network of roads leading from your eyes, ears, mouth, skin and joints. The roads terminate in different parts of the brain. Vehicles of all shapes and sizes are carrying a load of information about what is going on at the place they started. The eyes are bringing all they see, the skin every touch or scratch and the ears every little sound in the environment. When they reach their designated parking place in the brain, they open their doors, deposit their sensory load and then go back for more.

Integration

Our brain takes this sensory information and integrates it into a coherent response by linking up the different sites in the brain. The eyes check the information the ears have heard; the movement centre double-checks with the skin and eyes. The body uses this information to adapt the response it gives. The brain tells the body if the touch was a spider and if it needs to run or if the touch was your scarf brushing against your arm. The eyes double-check if the bang was a balloon or a falling roof beam. This is how your body knows if it is safe and can continue doing what it was doing – in the case of the party, playing with friends or sipping that wine. This is what we call an adaptive response. As Kranowitz (2005) says, the more accurate the information is, the better the response will be. You can see how a seemingly small difficulty processing sensory information can make life tricky. Understanding how your child's brain works will better equip you to help them.

Modulation

Our brains are ready and alert all the time, waiting for the information to come along the neural roads from all over the body. The brain acts like a sieve (see the next section) in that it tells us what we should take notice of and act on or what we can ignore. Simply put, the brain inhibits irrelevant sensory input so we can focus on what is important. Our primary need as humans is to stay safe and, on a very basic level, sensory input is used to tell us if we are in danger or not. As babies, we are aware of every sensation coming our way because we cannot keep ourselves safe but as we grow, our brains learn to ignore most sensory input and focus on what is needed to learn, love, have fun and ultimately survive. If we noticed every single sensory signal, we would be so overwhelmed we would not be able to function properly. What our brains and bodies are excellent at doing is habituating sensory input; in other words, noticing what we need and getting used to the rest and so ignoring it.

For example, when you put on a pair of skinny jeans, you feel the pressure of them on your skin for the first little while. The information from your skin is sent down the superhighway of tactile input to your brain and yells at you, 'These jeans are TIGHT!'

Your brain takes this yelling and cross-references it with information already stored inside you. It remembers that you look good in skinny jeans, you like this new pair and although they are not as comfy as your PJs you can cope for the sake of beauty. So, your brain sieves out what it doesn't need and holds on to what is needed – it sieves out the tactile input and holds on to how good you feel wearing those jeans.

A problem happens with modulation when our responses to input are consistently disproportionate to the input (Bundy, Lane & Murray 2002) – when that pair of tight jeans causes you discomfort all day so that eventually you can't focus on anything but the yelling from your skin.

Our brain, the sieve

What does this problem with modulating sensory input look like?

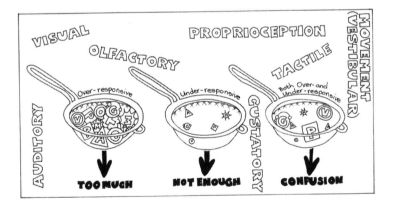

We can over-respond or be defensive to input (too tight, too loud, too bright) or we can be under-responsive to input (I need more movement, more spice on my food, louder music). Imagine the brain as a sieve. Information is brought to our brain from outside and inside our bodies (detection) and then integrated to form a response.

When we over-respond, a small amount of sensory information fills our brain up and it has a disproportionate effect. Typically, this will be seen in over-responsiveness to light or unexpected touch, noise, some visual input such as a cluttered classroom or certain smells and tastes. In some cases, people can be over-responsive to movement, for example, getting car sick quickly or becoming over-excited after jumping on the trampoline. And at the other extreme, we can be gravitationally insecure – a fear of movement or having your feet off the ground (Bundy et al. 2002).

Conversely, you may need more sensory information than others for you to register input and so your brain constantly seeks out more and more. It may be that you need to move more by running, jumping and crashing or hanging upside down off the sofa. You like extra spice on your food, or you like the TV on downstairs with the radio on upstairs while you read your book.

Often, we are both over- and under-responsive at the same time. For example, we need more movement than others but get easily overwhelmed by loud, busy places. This can be confusing as we seem loud and busy ourselves but then get quickly overwhelmed in spaces we seem to be similar with (Metz & Bolin 2019; Dunn 1997).

My daughter is a perfect example of this often-confusing picture. She is a sensory seeker, loves intense movement and is often bouncing around the house, singing loudly, and leaving a trail of chaos in her wake. When her neurodiverse friends visit, the noise levels become ear deafening as they chat and laugh, hugging and dancing around the kitchen.

But going to a local market that is loud, busy and full of the same intense sensory input, she can become quickly overwhelmed and freeze up. You might find her standing in a corner with her hands over her ears and tears streaming down her face. It feels like a contradiction; she is by nature loud and sensory seeking but is quickly pushed out of her window of tolerance in some spaces.

30 seconds to experience it

How does your own brain sieve sensory information? Do you over- or under-respond to sensory input? Are you easily overwhelmed by loud, busy places? Do you need to move all the time, fidget in long meetings, feel an urge to get up and move? Think about your child – are they over- or under-responsive? Does your booming voice push them out of their window of tolerance or does their constant movement feel too much for you? Reflect on how your sensory needs and their sensory needs balance each other out or tip each other over.

Chapter 3

What Happens When Our Brain Can't Process All the Sensory Information?

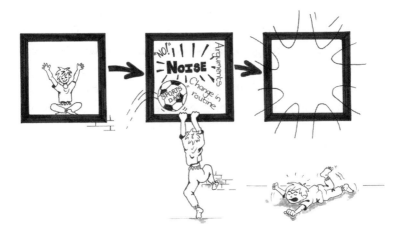

The family is excited about the school fair although the forecast predicts rain. This will mean all the stalls and fairground games are moved from the outside playground into the school hall. There is less space to move and an echo from the high roof which amplifies the sound. A brief discussion among ourselves and a decision is made that Daddy will stay at home this time. He is over-responsive to sound and unexpected touch. His ability to tolerate loud places with many people is small already but add the indoor space and the fact he has a big deadline at work causing stress equals a recipe for meltdown.

Put another way, his window of tolerance for the sensory input and what he perceives as the chaos of a school fair is small. Add additional stress of his work deadline to the mix and his window shrinks even further.

The window of tolerance is a term developed by Dr Dan Siegel to describe the perfect state of arousal in which we can function to the best of our ability (Siegel 2020). It is a great way of visualising what happens in our brains when we move in and out of what we can tolerate. When we are in our window of tolerance we can play, learn, work. We can be curious about the world, communicate with others and be the best version of ourselves. When we move out of our window of tolerance, our brains go into hyperarousal (fight or flight) or hypoarousal (dissociate or freeze). We will look at these states in more detail soon.

When we are out of our window of tolerance, we stop feeling safe.

Importantly, though, when we are inside our own window of tolerance, we can help others stay in theirs. We remain curious about what is happening for the other person; we can think of ways that might help them. When we are in our window, we are able to stay calm and connect with the other person, which helps them back into their window of tolerance. Conversely, when we are hanging out of our window and holding on with our fingertips, it is hard to connect with another human and co-regulate. We tend to pull each other out of our window of tolerance.

30 seconds to experience it

Have you ever noticed how much more difficult dinner or bath time or a day out can be if one of the adults has had a tough day and is tired? When trying to manage a tricky moment with your child, have you ever looked up at the other adult in the situation and commented that it might be better for them to go and calm down first? Does the room feel lighter and brighter when someone you love is feeling happy and in a good mood?

The way we process sensory input is unique to each of us. We all have unique triggers that can push us out of our window of tolerance and into fight, flight or dissociate. The sensory loads that our brains can tolerate change depending on many factors. What we can tolerate today we may not be able to tolerate tomorrow. It is the reason why at times our children remain a mystery to us. We feel we have worked out what triggered their strong reaction and then the next time it is different. We forget we are exactly the same. When I am excited about my day ahead, I have had a good night's rest and a filling breakfast, I will turn the music up in my car and bounce along the road, singing along. However, if I am worried about a meeting coming up, my sleep is poor and I am hungry, then I turn the music off as soon as I get in the car. My tolerance for sound changes depending on the day.

Let us think of a few aspects that may change the size of our window of tolerance. Remember, we are trying to build a picture of what is happening for our child as well as for ourselves. The sensory system is only one piece of the puzzle.

Co-morbid diagnosis

Although sensory processing difficulties can appear in isolation, they often co-exist with another diagnosis. It is imperative to consider the whole picture and not focus on sensory processing alone.

For example, if your sensory difficulties are part of autism, then you may find there are other aspects of life that can push you out of your window, such as changes in routine or transitioning from one activity to another. You may find sensory difficulties in autism, attention deficit disorders, mental health diagnosis, premature babies, people who have experienced trauma and neurological disorders such as cerebral palsy. This is not an exhaustive list; it helps to keep an open mind and explore the whole picture.

Sensory-based triggers

You may be *over-responsive* to sensory input, such as very often light or unexpected touch, noise, visual input or certain smells and tastes. We can also over-respond to movement.

Alternatively, you may be *under-responsive* to sensory input, for example needing to move (*vestibular input*) or engage in heavy muscle work (*proprioceptive input*) to feel regulated, needing to touch everything or chew on non-food items. When we are unable to meet, or prevented from meeting these sensory needs in an age-appropriate and safe way, it can push up anxiety and stress.

Masking how you are experiencing sensory input causes exhaustion, anxiety and shrinks our window of tolerance. This happens when a child or adult tries hard to hide their need to move or how overwhelmed they are by the environment. Often this happens in school or at work where there is pressure to conform. Parents often report the consequence to be a massive meltdown as soon as their child gets home after school.

When your *proprioceptive system* (movement sense) is not giving your body the information it needs to plan and execute movements (seen when you have dyspraxia or other movement-based disorders), it can be exhausting. Using cognition – that is, thinking about how to move and how much pressure to use instead of it being automatic – can cause increased stress and anxiety. Remember how much brain power it took not to puncture the paper in Chapter 1?

Low muscle tone due to an immature *vestibular system* (movement sense) can affect learning and life. You may struggle with fine motor skills such as writing, holding your posture, for example sitting upright in a chair, or holding your body up against gravity. This can be tiring and frustrating; for example, the child becomes upset when they have to write sentences for homework and you are convinced they are more than capable of creating the sentences in their mind but just can't put idea to paper.

The way our *sensory systems fit together* matters too. Families are made up of unique individuals with unique ways of processing sensory input. This might mean one of you is sensory seeking, loud and on the move most of the day while another of you is quickly overwhelmed by all that movement and noise. This is important to consider so that you can make sure everybody gets what they need to stay in their window of tolerance. The person who is over-responsive needs a quiet space to retreat to and the under-responsive person needs access to the input that calms their system.

Physiological and emotional state

Sleep, food and stress change how much you can tolerate, even if you don't have difficulty modulating sensory information.

Maslow's Hierarchy of Needs firmly places our physiological needs being met at the base of our ability to live a full life. Of course, I will assume that most of us reading this book have regular access to clean water, food and a safe place to sleep. However, when these needs are not met properly, for example high stress levels preventing you from having a good night's rest or you are too busy to eat properly, this has a direct impact on how your brain can modulate sensory input. Children who struggle to get enough sleep can be close to the edge of the window most of their day. As we move towards adolescence, our melatonin (sleep hormone) is secreted later than before. This means that teenagers struggle to fall asleep early enough yet they still need a good eight to ten hours of sleep. Being sleep-deprived will shrink their window of tolerance even further.

Think of a perfect work and school day. What does yours look like? The details will be different for us all but there are some basic, physiological needs that underlie much of our routines that we all will recognise. Might it be wonderful if you wake rested when the alarm goes off because you have had enough sleep? You get to drink your favourite drink and have enough time to take a warm shower without the kids fighting in the background. How about managing to eat something you enjoy that also feeds your body well and sets your sugar levels up for the morning?

The whole morning routine would be much harder if you were worried about the bills that are due and you know the bank account is empty. Or worse still, how would your morning routine be changed if you were worried it was the bailiff at the door when the postman knocks?

When you are experiencing times of heightened emotional states, your cortisol and adrenaline levels rise. When this happens, you can fall out of your window much more easily. At times, the emotional upheaval can be obvious, such as experiencing friendship difficulties at school or the death of a pet. However, our sensory children often are sensitive to life and will find some situations or times more difficult to process than others.

30 seconds to reflect

When you are tired and hungry at the end of a long day, how well do you manage a meltdown? What are some physical or emotional states that shrink your window of tolerance, for example lack of sleep or stress? What do you use to increase your window of tolerance? Examples could be going to the gym or having a long, hot bath.

Bonus 30 seconds to reflect

I am sure you can identify times when you are under higher pressure or when you are not able to give yourself the care you need. This could make you less able to manage the trickier times of the day with your sensory child. Think of small ways you could help yourself stay in your window of tolerance – eat regularly, take a walk to clear your head, call a friend, drink the tea while it is warm. Often it only takes a small act to help keep you grounded.

★ *Chapter 4* ★

What Happens When We Move Out of Our Window of Tolerance?

You have gone to visit your parents with your sensory teenager. Your mother insists that everyone sit at the table for lunch until they are excused by her when she feels the meal is over. This is super tricky for your teen as she is sensory seeking, the meal is taking forever, and you can see she is trying hard to sit still. The food has just been brought to the table when you spy your teen beginning to squirm in her seat. From experience, you know that a natural, mini movement break will help her regulate and you are about to ask her to fetch you a glass of water so she can move, when she stands up abruptly and announces loudly that she needs to use the toilet. Her tone is irritated as she is beginning to move out of her window of tolerance. What your mother instantly says is, 'Why are you being so rude?' She applies a moral stance to the behaviour, implying that your daughter is choosing to be rude. You know she is not being rude but really needs to move to regulate. Your mother has little understanding of SPD even though you have tried to teach her. Then she adds, 'If you could just sit still a little longer, then you could have had ice-cream but I guess you don't want any.' She is applying a top-down consequence, implying that if your daughter could just try harder to sit still then she could have a reward but if she can't then she loses a privilege.

We use these types of approaches across our lives. Classrooms have charts where children's names are moved up or down so they get rewarded for 'behaving' or punished for being naughty. We use sticker charts or marble jars to influence behaviour. We often suggest rewards for being good or doing well. This type of cognitive, top-down approach can be very successful for some children, even our sensory kids. However, they imply that the child can choose a different way of reacting to earn a reward. When we parent a sensory child, we need to reflect continually on when to use a top-down approach or when to try something different to help our child succeed.

Once we understand what is really happening for our sensory child when they move out of their window of tolerance, we might understand that these approaches can often set them up to fail or feel shame. Taking time to understand the way our brain and body work will help us build empathy for ourselves and our children. Empathy and compassion change the tone of our interactions with other humans.

To really begin to grasp what happens when we leave our window of tolerance, we require a little more understanding of our nervous system. Dr Stephen W. Porges, a Distinguished University Scientist at Indiana University, has gifted us with a wonderful model to visualise what happens when we move out of our window of tolerance. He calls it polyvagal theory (Porges 2011) and it provides us with a framework to recognise the cues our brains and bodies are giving and provides clues as to what we can do to help.

What happens in our brain?

Let me start with a story to help illustrate what Dr Porges has discovered about our brains.

The night before my sister's wedding in South Africa, I was getting ready for bed when a hysterical voice called for me from the other room. Going over to investigate, I found my sister stranded in the middle of her bed. An enormous, hairy spider had taken up residence in the bathroom. As it was her wedding day in the morning, I had little choice but to try and get rid of the monster so she could rest. I had to pretend to be brave for her sake. My body instantly told my brain that we were in grave danger, my heart rate shot up, my palms became sweaty and my head fuzzy. I was hyper-aware of all the sounds and movement in the room, even startling at the net curtain moving in the window.

Scanning the room for a weapon, a shoe caught my eye, but I abandoned the idea due to the sound crushing a huge spider might make. The spider was beginning to look more agitated every time I moved. I feared my heart was beating so loudly that it would antagonise the spider even further.

My sister, the terrified bride to be, was not helping the situation. She sat whimpering on the bed, occasionally letting out a little yelp. Her tone of voice and her fear seemed to seep into my brain making it even more foggy.

Had Sir David Attenborough been standing next to me telling me that this species of spider was not dangerous I would not have been able to do anything about my fear response. I was in fight mode and not able to listen to reason, no matter how sensible. The spider, although huge, was harmless, yet my body was telling me that we were in great danger.

This experience was pushing me way out of my window of tolerance!

What happened in my body and brain first? The starting place is called neuroception, the unconscious and involuntary reaction my body had to the spider.

Neuroception tells us if we are safe so we can continue to play, work, learn and love, or if we are in danger and need to get ready to do something to stay safe.

Deb Dana, the author of *The Polyvagal Theory in Therapy*, describes this as a wordless experience (Dana 2018). It happens without us being conscious of the process.

Neuroception listens to three messages from our nervous system:

★ What the *inside of our body* is telling us (the spider in the bathroom made my heart race, my palms sweat and my head feel fuzzy – which are all cues of danger).

★ What the *outside environment* is telling us (that the spider was huge and potentially dangerous and that we were stuck inside a small bathroom – all signs of danger).

★ How our *nervous system is always in relationship with another nervous system*, gathering information from them, scanning them for messages of danger or safety (this was my sister, frozen in the middle of the bed and yelping – all these cues giving me more information about the danger of the situation).

Before our brains can make meaning of what we are experiencing, our body already tells us what to do: fight the spider, run from the spider, or sit on the bed like my sister, frozen and whimpering. Just to let all spider lovers know, I managed to coax the spider into a bin, cover it with a magazine and run like a crazy person to the front door where I threw the whole lot out. The next morning, our father nearly tripped over the bin as he stepped out of the door.

Our brains and body communicate with information from inside, outside and another human and decide how to respond without time for perception or the ability to name and make meaning of our response. I wasn't stopping and thinking,

'Gosh I feel sweaty and sick, I must be afraid right now. I should really stop and look up a few facts about this spider before I make a plan on how to proceed.'

No, I simply felt and then acted.

Our primary need as human beings is to be safe. We can all relate to an irrational fear we might have. Most of us recognise that feeling of danger even when we know cognitively that we are physically safe, for example standing on a high bridge when you are afraid of heights.

When our children are pushed out of their window of tolerance by their sensory needs, their bodies might be telling them that they are in danger when they are physically not. A little like my body did with the spider.

Johnny is already worried before he even walks through the school gate because today is Tuesday, when they have music lessons in the hall. His tummy had felt funny at breakfast, so he hadn't eaten much but Mum said he had to go to school. Now, the lesson has started, and he is trying hard to understand what the teacher is saying. It is impossible because the hall echoes and the sound is so loud. Plus, he never gets to sit next to Billy in music even though Billy is his best friend.

The teacher is from another school, so she doesn't know that Johnny needs her to talk a bit slower and give him the chance to practise. His class teacher usually asks the whole class to practise new actions once first so she can see if everyone has understood what she means. Not this teacher, she just gets annoyed with him for not being able to follow the instructions like the others.

He is trying to watch Billy so he can copy him but the cymbals and the drums are too loud and he can't focus. Billy is too far away. He can feel his heart start to race, and his tummy feels yucky. Johnny is just about holding it together and then he looks over and sees the teacher frowning at him. He has no choice, his legs stand him up, he throws the stupid drum on the floor and runs out of the room to the toilet. Here it is quiet and small, so he hides away until his favourite teacher comes to find him.

Johnny's nervous system was already receiving cues of danger from his body before school started. His memory of previous lessons was triggering anxiety. When the music lesson started, his auditory system was quickly overloaded by the loud echoey hall and the drums. His brain was still trying to modulate the input and give him the opportunity to find safety when the third and final bit of information was received. His nervous system was searching for a cue of safety from the teacher, but she appeared annoyed with him for not focusing on her instructions. The message to Johnny's nervous system was loud and clear: he was in trouble. This was the final straw, pushing him out of his window of tolerance and into flight.

Johnny was not able to tell an internal story to help soothe his nervous system. He could not reason with himself about why the teacher might be frustrated or that the noise would stop soon.

Neuroception comes first. It tells your body what the state of safety is. It does not tell the story of what is happening to make any sense of it; it simply reacts. What we need to remember with our sensory children is that the messages their body are getting are not being processed like they should. This will mean that their worlds often don't feel safe even though they are safe.

Johnny was not in any danger during his music lesson, but he *felt* unsafe. This is exactly the same as my spider experience. I *felt* danger even though I was safe.

What happens after neuroception?

Dr Porges gives us the science for the ancient story of our brain's evolution through time. Over hundreds of thousands of years, humans have evolved so that we could survive and thrive as a species. The oldest part of our brain immobilises us so that we play dead in the face of a predator. We now call this dissociation or freeze. Later, we learned to run from our enemies or to fight them off. And finally, our mammalian brains evolved to enable us to seek out relationships with others and create community, what we will call social engagement (Porges 2011).

Deb Dana (2018) and Dr Porges suggest a helpful way of visualising what happens to our brains and body when we move out of our window of tolerance and no longer feel safe. They describe the process from top to bottom, just as it mirrors what happens in our brains. Thinking of how our bodies respond as we move from the top parts of our brain down to the most ancient can help us build empathy for ourselves and our children. This way we can view 'behaviours' with more depth and understanding.

At the top is social engagement, which we seek out first to feel safe. The ability to seek out another human for safety sits in the very top parts of our brain. If connection with another human is not enough to help us feel safe, we move down to the middle part of our brain which triggers our fight or flight. If fighting or running still does not help us feel safe, we move right down into the lower parts of our brain, and our bodies play dead to survive (we dissociate or freeze).

Social engagement

The newest part of our brains, the mammalian system, is all about connection. Science tells us that a connection to our mother is already being created inside her womb. We get to know the sound of her voice, the way she moves. Our brain begins to form a connection with our mother.

We are born with an innate need for other humans. Babies can't survive on their own. They rely on an adult to provide for their physical needs to survive. They can't feed or clean themselves. We now know too that babies need to build a relationship with a significant other in order to thrive. Meeting only basic physiological needs such as food and warmth is not enough for a baby to develop and grow. We all need connection.

Our nervous systems are continually seeking out others to help us feel safe. Our brains do not exist in isolation but in relationship with other brains. We scan humans for safety conveyed through their tone of voice, body posture, facial expressions and eye contact.

This is what we call social engagement, and it is the first place we seek out comfort when we are not feeling safe.

Let's go back to Johnny. It is likely that his cortisol levels were already high at breakfast time. The clues might have been found in his appetite being affected and his thought patterns circling around the music lesson coming up. His brain was collecting information from the filing cabinet of memories regarding the hall and how sound echoes in it, the teacher and her poor understanding of what he needed to succeed and the volume of a music lesson. We could hypothesise that social engagement could have changed how this lesson ended for him. Had Johnny been allowed to sit next to Billy who knew him well, this could have given him a feeling of connection with some-one. Remember the experiment by Dr Coan we discussed in the introduction? He discovered that we experience less pain when we are with someone who cares for us. Being alongside a person we trust can help us feel better. Had the teacher reflected on her non-verbal communication and smiled encouragingly at Johnny instead of frowning, this might have given him enough social connection to feel able to stay in the lesson. However, all this might not have been enough for his nervous system to feel calmed. His nervous system may already have been too close to the edge for human connection to help.

When social engagement can't give us what we need to feel safe, we become mobilised to keep ourselves safe another way. We move down towards fight or flight. This might happen when the sensory overload is too much for us to navigate through social connection alone. It might be that we are continually in a heightened state of stress; the cortisol levels in our body are high and not coming down to healthy levels often enough. When we are in this state, it might only take a small event to push us into fight or flight.

Co-regulation and self-regulation

In the West, we have high expectations on our children to learn to self-regulate from a young age. Books have been published for parents of new-born babies that give tips on how we can teach them to self-soothe and not need our help to calm down. Of course, we want our children to learn to self-regulate and find ways to manage their sensory needs. However, science tells us that social engagement is our first stop for safety; we need another human to teach us how first. This underpins why we first need to teach children to regulate with us first (co-regulation) before they are able to do it on their own.

Regulation is a two-way process

Co-regulation begins at birth when a baby cries and the parent picks the child up to soothe them. The parent might gently rock the baby and use a calm, even tone of voice telling the baby they are OK. The baby feels the calm presence of the parent, hears the tone of voice and the rocking, and begins to feel calm.

This cycle is not one way, though. The parent might feel their stress rise when the baby cries. They may be tired and feeling a little out of control too, as they are caring for a small, new baby. However, the rocking and weight of the baby in their arms are calming to the parent too. As the baby begins to calm, the parent gets a shot of good hormones to the brain and begins to feel calmer as well.

It does feel good to soothe a crying baby, doesn't it?

So, it is a cycle of co-regulation; the baby learns to feel safe as the adult caring for them learns how to help them feel safe.

We help each other feel better.

This cycle of co-regulation is important to remember as we learn to help our sensory children to regulate.

We always need to learn to co-regulate with our child before we can expect them to self-regulate.

Fight/flight

The next part of the brain to evolve was the sympathetic nervous system, which floods our body with cortisol and adrenaline. If being in connection with another person to co-regulate with doesn't work, then we go into defence and protect ourselves by running away or by fighting to stay safe. When we move into fight or flight, we can no longer think clearly or reason. No matter if it is true or not, we go into a state of survival and are prepared to yell, punch, throw or run our way through the threat.

Think of our baby again. When they start to feel a little hungry, they have some non-verbal cues they will employ to try and get food from an adult, such as rooting their head to the side, trying to latch on to something and maybe using their voice a little. If nobody comes to give the baby the food, survival instinct will kick in, and they will become louder and shout until food arrives.

There are many reasons why the connection with another human may not be enough to prevent the fall into fight or flight (think back to our window of tolerance). What is important to hold on to here is that we can still use our social engagement system and connection to help someone out of this state or prevent them from falling further down towards dissociation.

Freeze/dissociate

When we fall further we move into freeze or dissociation. The oldest part of our brain is the parasympathetic nervous system and it evolved to keep animals and humans safe by playing dead. This immobilisation was created to confuse prey by slowing the heart rate down and making the body lie very still as though dead. Moving down into this part of our brain will send us into dissociation or freeze. Our heart rate drops, we might feel cold and we disengage. On an extreme level, we may lose consciousness. We may feel separated from the world, and some describe the feeling as floating above your body. We feel disconnected and far away (Dana 2018).

30 seconds to experience it

Try the *still face experiment* with someone (Tronick 2007). Sit facing each other. Now take turns: one of you talk for 30 seconds about anything at all, for example your favourite holiday, book or what you did last week. The other person should listen but keep their facial expression totally blank; do not smile, encourage or nod. Be a very poor listener. It might help to look down at your phone and simply glance up occasionally. Each person takes a turn to listen and to talk.

How did it feel when you got no feedback from the person who was listening to you? What happened with your neuroception? Did you start to become more animated, try to make the story bigger and better to try and gain the attention of the person listening? This is the use of social engagement to get a person to connect with what you are telling them and help you to feel safe. Did you begin to feel annoyed or frustrated with the person who was listening? Did you feel your voice rising and anger stirring until eventually, you just felt like getting up and leaving? This is a fight or flight response kicking in. Or finally, did you start to feel anxious and stumble over your words? Did you begin to find it impossible to think of what you wanted to say at all, even though you were simply retelling a story you know well? Did you feel as if you would prefer to stop talking and give up? This is dissociation beginning, where your brain is shutting down to keep you safe.

The disconnect: top-down vs bottom-up

When we move down from social engagement to fight, flight or freeze, our thinking brain can no longer function. Our cortex, the part of our brain we use to problem solve, use language or understand consequences, disconnects from our lower brain. We go into survival mode.

When we are here, our nervous system is not able to access reason. Remember my reaction to the spider? I was beyond reasoning; I was simply reacting.

Johnny had no choice but to stand up, throw that drum and run to a place of safety. His body took over and his ability to think it through disappeared.

The thinking brain disconnects when we go into fight, flight or freeze. Fawn is another way that our brain can react when we move out of our window of tolerance. We can talk of fight, flight, freeze and fawn. When we fawn, we try to please and become compliant, even when we don't want to be, so that we avoid any conflict. We will not look at fawn in detail in this book as it is more typically seen in those of us who have experienced trauma and is best discussed in that context.

30 seconds to experience it

Dr Dan Siegel gives us a wonderful, visual way of remembering this in his book, *The Whole-Brain Child* (Siegel & Bryson 2011). Hold your hand in a fist with your thumb tucked in. The outside of your hand is the cortex, your thinking brain. You can reason here, make decisions based on facts, solve problems and make a choice about what you are going to do. Your thumb, tucked in under your thinking brain is your limbic system. This is where fight, flight or freeze are activated. As Dr Siegel says, this is where all your big emotions live. Now lift your fingers up, keeping your thumb tucked into your palm. When you get pushed out of your window of tolerance, your thinking brain flips up and disconnects from your limbic system. Now your fight, flight or freeze response is in control. You can't think your way out of the situation until top and bottom are reconnected.

As a society, our 'go to' strategy for modifying behaviour is cognitive or moral. We use rewards or consequences to help keep things in order. These work well for some of us. I go to work so I can get paid. I drive within the speed limit to prevent a fine. My daughter puts her hand up in class and waits her turn to speak so her name doesn't get moved onto the cloud or into the red on the 'behaviour wall chart' in class.

What happens when your thinking brain disconnects from your lower brain and you simply can't comply with expectations?

Let's apply some cognitive strategies to what happened with Johnny. His mother could have anticipated a tricky music lesson due to the phone call last Tuesday detailing a similar outcome. She might have sat Johnny down at breakfast and suggested a reward for good behaviour in the music lesson.

'Johnny, if you can stay in the lesson today and not throw anything then I will take you to get an ice-cream after school. What do you think? Can you try?'

Johnny loves spending time with his mum as much as he loves ice-cream so will try harder today. We can hypothesise that one of two things might happen.

Scenario 1

Johnny will mask his sensory needs, push them down so he manages to stay in the lesson and not throw the drum. He will enlist every ounce of his energy and brain power to ignore all the cues of danger he is experiencing. This scenario will seem optimal for people looking in like the teacher, Johnny will stay in the lesson and the drum will not be broken. For Johnny, it will mean higher cortisol levels, pushing him closer to the edge of his window of tolerance. He will not learn anything in the lesson as he is using all his energy to stay calm. It is likely that the message he will hear from the adults is that he is just not trying hard enough; his meltdowns are therefore his fault. This increase in cortisol and adrenaline will not dissipate; they will need to go somewhere. Johnny might have a massive meltdown later when he is home and feeling safe (fight/flight). Or he might push it all down and become increasingly anxious and withdrawn (freeze/dissociate).

Scenario 2

Johnny may try to ignore his body but no matter how much he tries to stay in the lesson, his body simply can't do it. The scene plays out just as it did last week. Johnny loses that ice-cream. Both he and his mum feel like they have failed.

What about a third scenario?

Let's look at the brain again.

Sensory input is received from the cerebellum and feeds into the limbic system. This has a calming effect on the brain.

Imagine Johnny's brain as a bowl that fills up with sensory

input. The sieve is small and all that noise and anxiety begin to fill up and clog his brain. If we could find a way to tap it out, drain it from his brain then he might have enough to keep his brain connected and able to learn.

Using our sensory systems as a way to regulate can help our brain stay connected.

Giving Johnny access to sensory strategies to feed into his brain and calm it may prevent him from having a meltdown. Using a bottom-up approach first will help Johnny regulate so he can use a top-down strategy to stay in the lesson. We will spend time later in the book looking at how to use our sensory systems to regulate but let's think of a few for Johnny now. Ear defenders could help with the noise (auditory), getting Johnny to move, for example, being the one who hands out the musical instruments or asking the whole class to get up and stomp to the rhythm of the drum (vestibular and proprioceptive), a weighted lap pad while sitting (tactile), and knowing he is allowed to get up and remove himself to a different space if it all gets too overwhelming. And lastly, giving him instructions one at a time with a moment to process and a physical demonstration of what is expected (auditory and proprioceptive) will also help.

You may be tempted to flick ahead to the chapter with sensory regulating suggestions and be perplexed to find a whole bunch of chapters focused on you instead. It all has to do with the social engagement system. Remember that connection with another person is the foundation for feeling safe and so that is why we focus on ourselves first.

★ *Chapter 5* ★

How Our Brains Are Connected to Each Other

Before we move on to reflecting on how we ourselves manage our children's sensory needs and our own window of tolerance, let us look at one more scientific phenomenon, the mirror neuron.

A yawn is contagious, right? When we walk into a coffee shop and the barista is friendly, makes eye contact, smiles and asks after your day, you might walk away feeling happier than when you arrived. How about a meal where everyone is laughing and joking when a tired, stressed person arrives home?

Does the atmosphere at the dinner table change when they sit down with their grumpy face?

Scientists accidentally discovered mirror neurons in the 1990s. They had monkeys hooked up to an MRI (magnetic resonance imaging) scanner, studying what parts of the brain light up when they open and eat nuts. At lunchtime, the hungry scientist went to snack on a nut, cracking it open and popping it in his mouth. The monkey, still hooked up to the MRI, watched him steal his nuts and eat them. To the scientist's surprise, the monkey's brain lit up in the same place while watching the scientist open and eat a nut as it did when it was eating nuts itself. The first mirror neuron ever detected was due to a snacking scientist (Taylor 2016).

What they had uncovered was a fascinating brain fact. When you perform an action, for example biting into a sour lemon, the same neurons that light up in your brain will light up in mine. I might anticipate the tough texture of the skin and my own mouth may fill with saliva while I watch you experience the sourness of the lemon. Our brains mirror each other. When you yawn, I might yawn. When you frown, I might frown. Dr Dan Siegel suggests that mirror neurons are the reason second or third siblings are sometimes better at sports than the first – they have had more time watching their brother or sister play a sport and their mirror neurons have been firing over and over making it easier for them to learn (Siegel & Bryson 2011).

Mirror neuron lesson 1

Your children are watching you and their brains are firing just like yours. When you are gentle with the cat, help the neighbour to carry her bags into the house, smile at the bus driver, slam the door in anger, shout to be heard or swear at the bus driver, their brains are firing in the same way. They are learning from you all the time.

Mirror neurons form part of the understanding that our brains do not exist in isolation but rather in connection with other brains. As we explored in the earlier chapter, we are continually scanning other humans for cues of safety. Social baseline theory and polyvagal theory both tell us the story of how we bounce our emotions off each other; if you are angry, sad or filled with joy, my brain fires in the same way alongside yours. That is why emotions are contagious. When I come back from a relaxing weekend away with my girlfriends, ready to share the hilarious stories of our antics but am met with the miserable face of my husband who has had to deal with melt-downs all weekend, I will feel my joy dissipate. But it can go the other way too. Last week I became overwhelmed at work with too many people asking me too many questions at once. A colleague simply came over to me, spoke to me with a calm tone, made gentle eye contact and smiled while telling me to go and have a cup of tea and she would sort it all out. Now, the offer of help was wonderful but what really changed my state from stressed to calm was the way my brain began to fire with hers. Her calm voice and face sent me cues of safety, the connection to her underpinned that, and my mirror neurons fired with hers.

Mirror neuron lesson 2

You are a powerful tool for helping your child regulate. Yes, there are some fantastic sensory tools you can use, but your biggest asset is you and your brain! Your body language, tone of voice and facial expressions can change the way your child is feeling. Simple and powerful.

My daughter found sitting still and focusing for any length of time near impossible. This became more of an issue for her as she came closer to important exams in her teens. She was and still is a sensory-seeking young person who needs intense and regular heavy muscle work and movement to learn. Her body and brain simply cannot learn without it. However, she was not always aware of what she needed, often forgetting that her frus-tration with studying was partly due to her sensory needs. I also regularly forgot, especially when I was becoming frustrated with her apparent lack of motivation; trying to get a teenager to sit and study when they are literally jumping around the room can do that! These moments were a recipe for disaster. My body language and tone of voice conveyed annoyance even as I gave her access to the sensory tools that might help.

'Go and jump on the trampoline for ten minutes,' said with a calm, understanding tone or growled out of a deep irritation had a totally opposite effect on her. Obviously. The science backs this up. Her brain mirrors mine and we either help each other through the moment or we pull each other further away from the desk with the books and pens. My body and brain were nearly more powerful than the sensory strategy.

This is the part of the story that is often hard for us to have to accept: when we are the parent then we have to be more in control than we ever feel capable of. I wish it wasn't that way but it is.

There is good news though. Thinking about how interconnected our emotions are may seem so obvious now as you read this but how will we even know how or where to start? We will journey through some of this in Part 2. We can learn how to connect and communicate with our children in a new way. It might take time and some effort but it is worth it when we learn how powerful our own state can be.

ANIMAL ANALOGIES
Learning and Reflecting on How We React to Our Sensory Child and Why It Matters

Chapter 6

Why Use Animal Analogies?

The day I knew I was going to become a mother was the day the guilt began to seep into my life. We are our own harshest critics and the language we use with ourselves matters. There is enough language around us, especially when it comes to parenting a child with sensory needs, that helps feed our own guilt and self-blame! Why add more?

As a family, we first came across these animal analogies in a book called *Skills-based Learning for Caring for a Loved One with an Eating Disorder* (Treasure, Smith & Cane 2007). We were in the throes of trying to help our desperately ill teenager survive the grips of severe anorexia and were becoming increasingly aware that our tone of voice, our body language and our facial expressions either fed her anxiety or helped abate it.

Using animal analogies gave us a language for reflecting on how we were managing some very difficult moments. It was a way of reflecting that held less of the blame element and gave us a framework to think about how we were reacting to our child's needs in light of how we were feeling ourselves.

In Part 1 we firmly established our understanding of how important social engagement and connection is to humans. Looking at the brain has shown us that using sensory strategies will help our children regulate so they can love, play and learn. We have found that the most important piece of the puzzle is co-regulation and that we can't help someone regulate if we are not regulated ourselves. How we react and communicate can change how our child's brain perceives danger. We can feed into the fight, flight or freeze response and push them deeper towards meltdown. Or we can stand calmly on the edge of their emotions, a calm and safe space for them to come to when they are ready. We can create a space of connection where social engagement can occur.

When we ourselves are in fight, flight or fright/freeze, it is nearly impossible for us to use the top part of our brain, our cortex, to access coherent, rational thinking. Each animal we are looking at is a way of reflecting on what state your *own* brain and body are in. The jellyfish and kangaroo are often stuck in a state of fright or freeze, the rhino is in fight, the ostrich is dissociated. The dolphin and St Bernard have found strategies to connect their cortex to their limbic systems and they use social engagement effectively to create an atmosphere of connection and safety. You cannot help anybody else regulate and manage their strong emotions when you are way out of your own window of tolerance.

In Part 2, we will spend time reflecting on ourselves. We will look at how we connect with our children and how this is the starting point for our child to learn to regulate themselves.

Learning a new way of communicating is not as simple as 1, 2, 3 but it can be done. Our brains and bodies can learn more quickly than we think! These animal analogies are designed to help you find your strengths and give you tips on how to manage difficult moments.

It is important to remember a few things as you begin to read through the next chapters. First, as parents we do not have the characteristics of just one animal. We are bits of all of these concepts; sometimes we are more of one than the other. It all depends on where you are in your own window of tolerance. One day you may be more regulated and calm; you may have less on your to-do list and so you may be much more able to connect with your child and give their sensory systems what they need (a dolphin). The next day you may be tired and stressed so just simply do not have the emotional capacity for connection, so you raise your voice and threaten (a rhino). This should not be an exercise in self-blame or negativity. It is an opportunity to reflect and find what you are already doing well and think through what you can work on.

Before we move on to the animal analogies, here is one last thing to keep in mind. As you read through Part 2, try not to spend all your time trying to find other people in the chapters. If you fill up your mind with thoughts such as my partner is a jellyfish and my mother is a rhino, then you might miss seeing what you need for yourself. Try to read this book for yourself first and foremost before looking for others in the words.

Never forget that you are the strongest tool in the tool kit. A sensory strategy is only as powerful as the person who is offering it.

Chapter 7

Yellow Cars and Pregnant Ladies

You Notice What You Think About

Before we dive into the animal analogies, let's take a moment to reflect on what we think about, our thought patterns. I bought a small, bright yellow car last year. I named him Senor Custard. The car was supposed to be my statement of being unique and different but as soon as I made the decision to buy that little yellow car, I began seeing yellow cars everywhere. I had never noticed how many yellow cars there were in my neighbourhood until I started thinking about yellow cars. My car was not so unique after all!

Do you remember when you or your partner or your sister were pregnant? You began to notice pregnant women everywhere, and you may have thought, is everybody having a baby this year? Before your thoughts were filled with being pregnant and babies, you hardly noticed the baby bumps.

→ **Try this**
Dwell on what you have done well:

- ✓ Write the moments down in a notebook.
- ✓ Start a bead box – each bead represents a good moment (like a star chart for yourself).

✓ Photograph moments on your phone.
✓ Send yourself a text telling yourself what you did well.
✓ Call a friend and tell them.
✓ Tell your child what you did well.

We notice what we are thinking about, whether that is yellow cars and pregnant ladies, or something else entirely.

This is true for thought patterns of yourself as a parent – yes, even your thought patterns about your child.

If you think you are failing and doing badly, then you will notice those moments over all the others. You may not see the small, sometimes micro moments you are rocking it as a parent! What you believe about yourself changes how you approach a tough situation with your child. When the chaos hits and you have spent time thinking of how out of control you feel, then you will only notice the moments you are not coping. If you purposefully think about the times you have done well, then you may notice these first. If your thoughts centre around how painful and beyond fixing the problems in your relationship are then you will notice the times they are. If you consciously and purposefully focus on the times you and your child have joy and connection, even a small micro moment, you will see them again.

I challenge you to notice what you are thinking about. Try to see the moments you are rocking it as a parent!

And when you notice the moment your child makes your heart swell with love, write it down, take a photo, look back on it.

Dwell on it!

Keep this in mind as you begin to read through the animal analogies. If you are reading them through a lens of your failures, you will only find more failures. If you read them through a lens of what you are doing well, then you will see more of those moments.

★ *Chapter 8* ★

The Jellyfish

Highly attuned to the emotions of others, can be easily wobbled by them.

At its best, a jellyfish:

- ★ is finely attuned to their child's emotions and can read their body language very well
- ★ is able to mentalise (see the dolphin chapter for more on this) and know why they are reacting that way they are.

At its worst, a jellyfish:

- ★ is easily triggered by the emotions of the child. If the child is sad, the jellyfish becomes sad; if they are angry, the jellyfish's emotions rise up quickly
- ★ is swept up by the emotions of the child and feels out of control quickly.

It is nearly dinner time, and you are shopping with your child, going as fast as you can because it is too loud, too bright and he is tired and hungry. Come to think of it, so are you but you have no food he will eat in the house, so you have no choice. You feel yourself on edge already; shopping with your sensory child is a challenge at the best of times. As you put the eggs into the trolley, you hear the tell-tale change in your child's tone of voice. Perhaps it isn't his voice that changes but his facial features tell the 'impending meltdown' story. You see a woman standing by the bread shelves and notice that she is peering at you. What is she looking at, why do people always have to judge us when they have no idea how hard a simple shop for dinner can be? Your stomach flips, your heart rate goes up and you feel your emotions rise. You picture what might be about to happen, the floppy, screaming, snotty child tucked under your arm as you abandon your food and leave, wishing there was a back exit. Who needs food anyway? Your brain and body remember the last meltdown in the egg aisle. More than that, you can see that the hunger, loud music, fluorescent light and too many people are pushing your child out of his window of tolerance. You allow your child's rise in emotion to trigger a rise in yours.

Now the annoying thing is that as your emotions wobble, your child, finely attuned to you at this very moment (in the way you wish he was when dressing for school in the mornings but never is), begins to feed off your emotion. And you off theirs and they off yours and there it is – Meltdown City! To top it all off, the lady by the bread looks over again, making you feel even worse.

Jellyfish float about the ocean, beautiful and mesmerising but have you ever seen a jellyfish washed up on a beach? It collapses on itself and becomes a translucent puddle on the floor. Why? Because a jellyfish is a wobbly creature without a solid skeleton to hold it up. It has no backbone or any bone for that matter. I imagine that if you poked a jellyfish on one side, it would cause a Mexican wave of movement across the creature. A jellyfish does not hold the title for most stable of animals.

You may be asking, 'What on earth has this blob of jelly got to do with parenting?'

When we jellyfish (yes, I am turning a noun into a verb; call it creative licence), we allow our child's strong emotion to trigger in us a strong emotion. When they are upset, we become upset. When they are angry, we feel a strong reaction rise up in us. When they are panicked, we feel our own anxiety begin to rise.

When we jellyfish, we wobble in the face of our child's emotions.

It is natural for us to have an emotional reaction to our children's strong feelings. At our best when we jellyfish, we have empathy for our child. We have taken time to understand how they feel and have tried to imagine why they feel that way. We notice the small non-verbal cues, the tiny changes in their tone of voice or facial expression and we anticipate what is going to happen next. Being so attuned with our child moves us to do something when our child is upset. At our worst, this ability to read and anticipate what is coming causes us to feel out of control to some degree, to be overwhelmed by their emotion.

To jellyfish is to get on their wave of emotion with them and allow ourselves to be swept up with them. When we jellyfish, we allow our children's strong emotions to trigger ours.

Think back to what we have learned about our brains. When we jellyfish, we are absorbing the emotions of our child. They are not feeling in control so look to us for stability and safety. They scan your face and body for signs that they are going to be OK but if you are being triggered and becoming anxious yourself, then the cues they see simply echo what they already feel. It can cause a cycle that is tricky to get out of.

When we are tired, exhausted and emotionally depleted from caring for a child with sensory needs, our window of tolerance shrinks. This means we are more likely to be a jellyfish. Our kids require constant thought and attention, often simply to do things others take for granted. Attending their best friend's birthday party needs careful forward planning because it might be loud and busy. Choosing an after-school club most suitable for a child who finds gross motor skills frustrating takes mental effort. Making sure you have a healthy, crunchy snack in your handbag at school pick-up time so that your child can use their oral motor system to stay regulated on the way home needs forward planning. Explaining to the teacher why she should allow your child to move more in class is time consuming. So much thought and effort going into everyday tasks can be exhausting for you. Being tired can make us much more likely to jellyfish.

Those of us who jellyfish also often carry high levels of self-blame. My daughter struggled with the change from junior to secondary school. Moving from her small, nurturing school to a large school full of big kids was frightening. Her anxiety triggered anxiety in me. Would she be OK? Would they understand her needs? I could have reasoned that all humans find change tricky at times. Moving jobs is scary and moving schools is scary. But instead, I worried that her anxiety about change was actually because I had not given her enough tools to manage the change, that her anxiety was linked to my poor parenting. This self-blame fed my jellyfishing and in turn my anxiety.

What about you in the supermarket? You might be thinking, 'Why can't I control him? What am I doing wrong? Maybe my friend is right. I do need to be stricter!'

Fear is another emotion that fuels our inner jellyfish. In my case, when my daughter was transitioning schools, I feared she would not cope and that I in turn would not cope. The mum in the supermarket may be thinking, 'If I can't help you as a toddler then how on earth will I help you when you are 13?' Fear and the jellyfish are great friends!

If you are reading this and thinking, 'Yes, I jellyfish sometimes', don't feel alone. And don't be hard on yourself. The first step is simply to notice that sometimes you allow your child's emotions to wobble you. We are not trying to be perfect parents; we are taking time to reflect on what we already do well and do more of that!

Remember that being so finely attuned to your child's emotions can be positive too. You already know how they are feeling, sometimes before they even know themselves. Your skill at knowing when they need you and what for is what makes you able to help them. What a jellyfish needs to practise is how not to absorb that emotion and be thrown by it. At their best, a jellyfish has learned to regulate their own anxiety and stress so that they can be a stable and calm space for their child. It can be done! It requires some work and practice but our brains are amazing and we can learn a new way.

→ Try this

Burden bearers

Building a community of people around you that will help you carry the emotional burden is life giving. There are parents just like you, with similar stories. Find them online, at the school gate, at your church, and be vulnerable. Vulnerability is courage at its best. Be brave and open up to someone. You may be pleasantly surprised at the outcome.

So, you jellyfish sometimes. What can you do to help yourself?

Build a community

Connecting with others who 'get it' can be lifesaving. Surrounding yourself with other parents who are further along in the journey is a wonderful and scientifically proven way of helping equip yourself to do better. A study by Christakis and Fowler in 2011 looked at how important the community of people around you is and how it can influence you to succeed. The study looked at the spread of happiness and how one person's happiness can influence not only those closest to them to be happier but also their friends' friends too. They found a wonderful phenomenon. When you get happier, so does your neighbour and your neighbour's friend. In their book, *Connected*, Christakis and Fowler (2011) note that the spread of happiness is true for other parts of life too. For example, if your friend gets fitter by starting to use their gym membership, then you are statistically more likely to get fitter too. It doesn't end with you, though; another of your friends is more likely to start going to the gym too. Relationships such as marriages and parenting are influenced in the same way. If you are around parents who you connect with, who understand what you are dealing with and who are doing what you want to do more of, you will do better. And so will your friends. Surrounding yourself with people who are doing more of what you want to do is scientifically proven to help you to learn new skills. I see it in our parenting groups all the time. One parent will report back that they managed to stay calm in the face of a meltdown, and next week, others will report the same. Find a support group you can join locally or online. There are so many different groups you can look for, such as ADHD, autism and adoption support groups. Parents on our parenting course consistently feed back that simply being able to talk to others who understand made them feel stronger and more able.

Take time to reflect

Take time to reflect on what is triggering your reaction to your child's strong emotions. Ask yourself some tough questions. For example, are you feeling rejected by your child? Often their words can feel like a personal attack on you as a person or a rejection of your parenting. Does a part of you believe them when they shout, 'I hate you'? When our children struggle, we can feel like a failure as a parent and then their words appear to confirm what we feel. We can wonder if we are missing an important piece of the puzzle and not doing enough to help them reach their potential. Do you sometimes resent your child for taking up so much of your time and energy? We have all felt that at some point; don't feel guilty. Are you comparing yourself to the mother on the playground who looks as if she has it all together? Are you exhausted and overwhelmed? All of these will be more likely to shrink your window of tolerance and make it harder for you to deal with the tricky moments.

What could help ease your load

This is a statement that consistently gets a howl of frustration from parents. It feels impossible to prioritise anything other than your child in the face of real struggle and we often feel so alone that finding help seems impossible. Try to change your perspective. Understand that making sure you are feeling more in control and supported will have a direct impact on your child. Do you need to consciously plan more self-care into your week? Do you need to recruit some help around the house or with the children? Are you over committed and are there parts of your life you need to let go of for a while so you can care for yourself? Are you prioritising your health and your relationships, or have you let them slide to look after your child? It is not self-indulgent or selfish to care for yourself and it is not a failure to get more help if you need it. It is a responsible act of kindness to yourself that will ultimately help your child.

Looking after yourself and getting more help if you need it is not a luxury; it should be a top priority.

Be brave

Which of your friends or family members can you call up and ask to be your support buddy? You will be surprised by how honoured a person feels when you let them into your pain and ask them to support you. They don't need to give advice and have all the answers; they could simply make you a cup of tea and give you a tissue or listen over the phone. Having someone to lean on will make you stronger. Often, we don't talk about how much we are struggling, and we try to be strong. Real courage lies in being vulnerable with someone you trust and being honest about how tough parenting a sensory child can be.

Who speaks in your life

On that note, reflect on which people you are giving a voice to in your life – the ones you allow to have an opinion on your family. Do they understand what sensory needs your child has and how to help manage them? Do they believe in you as a parent? Do they give you positive words of affirmation? Do they challenge you gently and with love? If they don't, then you have the right to put in a boundary, asking them not to give their opinion unless asked. You can do this in a kind and loving way. Saying something like, 'I know you care deeply about me and my child and that you are trying to help by giving advice. It would really help me though if you wait until I ask for advice from you.' Perhaps you can give them this book so they can learn more about the needs your child has.

Simple mantras

Choose some simple mantras that you can recite when things start to go wrong. 'I am enough.' 'I am a good parent.' 'This too shall pass.' 'I am strong.' 'I am a survivor.' Put them on your phone screen, fridge door. These are truths and the more you say them the more likely you are to start believing them. If you believe you are a strong, fantastic parent, you are less likely to jellyfish.

Fact or fiction

Is what you are feeling based on the truth or is your brain changing it up for you? Catastrophising? Sometimes what we feel is based on truth, but it gets warped into a lie by our minds. For example, the child screaming on the supermarket floor may look like terrible, out-of-control parenting but we know the truth is that your child is in meltdown. A mother relayed an incident to me of her son having a particularly hard day. They were at the start of their journey towards understanding his sensory needs and he had become overwhelmed and way out of his window of tolerance. She noticed two older ladies watching as she and her husband wrestled her son into the car, howling and sad. She imagined they were judging her parenting but was deeply surprised when they approached her to tell her how amazing she was and how well they thought she was doing as a mother. The fiction in her head was that they were going to berate her and the fact was they were looking at what was happening with admiration and support. This changed her perspective completely, and after this she always considers that people around are thinking the best and not judging her.

Jellyfish in action

Let's go back to you in the supermarket. You and your son are feeding off each other's strong emotions and you are beginning to feel as overwhelmed as he is. What could you do to help you both? The obvious sensory strategies we could think of are not just valid for him but for you too. As parents, we are often so focused on making sure our child gets what they need that we forget that the sensory strategies will work for us too! Let's start with the oral motor system to try and keep them in their window of tolerance. Have something to drink with a straw, for example, a juice box for him and water bottle for you, grab a bag of crunchy carrots or crackers at the start of the shopping trip and both nibble on those (not forgetting to pay for them at the checkout!). Using the auditory system, perhaps use his noise-cancelling headphones or play two or three of your favourite songs on the phone and let him know that once the songs are done, the shopping trip will be over (a musical timer). The 'timer' can help you keep on track too, giving you the focus to get in and out faster. Music can also be regulating and calming. Use his body to ground him by asking him to push the trolley or jump over every line at the end of each aisle, or really focus on how pushing the trolley helps your body feel a little more grounded.

We know, though, that these strategies alone might not be enough when you are both tired and hungry. What could you do to help yourself not to jellyfish? You may be imagining the last time you were at the shops and it all ended badly. Perhaps you can try to remember a day all went as smoothly as it could have? Remember that we see what we focus on; think back to our yellow cars and pregnant ladies. I know this may sound fluffy, but it is science; if you were to start the shopping thinking, 'This will all end in disaster' versus 'I am able to get through this quickly and help him stay regulated' this may help your brain stay calm and your child's will mirror yours. What about that annoying old lady by the bread? Have we assumed she is judging and thinking badly of you? I have certainly done that! Perhaps, like our example earlier, we could wonder if she is watching you with a sense of admiration for how well you are doing. We can't know what she is thinking, can we, unless we ask.

Chapter 9

The Rhino

Fiercely loyal and protective of our families but can tend to control situations.

At its best, a rhino:

- ★ is deeply loyal and protective of their family
- ★ cares deeply and can be sensitive
- ★ is excellent at setting and holding a boundary using their tone of voice and body language without using fear or coercion.

At its worst, a rhino:

- ★ uses control and coercion to force children to behave in a different way
- ★ is misunderstood and labelled as being too harsh or a bully
- ★ uses their body and tone of voice to intimidate.

Bedtimes can create a perfect storm. You cooked dinner but your child wouldn't eat it because today they mysteriously don't like spaghetti any more, their favourite food of all time. You are exhausted from rushing between 100 jobs all day and very likely hungry because you fed your child without also nourishing yourself. You desperately want to sit and eat in peace, so you attempt bedtime with your own body needing the same care you are providing the children. Your child is exhausted after a long day at school and is in sensory overload. She is bouncing on the bed and talking incessantly at top volume, without drawing breath. She does not look sleepy at all! Your window of tolerance is shrinking fast. You try asking her to go to bed using your calm voice; you employ every tactic in your toolbox but nothing is working. In fact, you are pretty sure nothing is going to work and you are getting yourself ready for the battle that is charging towards you. Before you are even aware of it, you are out of your window of tolerance. Your inner rhino appears, you raise your voice and yell, 'Get into your bed now!' For good measure you add, 'If you don't get in the bed right now, then I will take all this Lego and throw it in the bin', as you reach towards the box. Your child stares at you mid bounce, slows down for a second and then the bouncing continues. Your anger rises. This is exactly what your mother was implying when she told you that you are too soft; they just will not listen to you, ever! You raise the volume of your voice, your face is angry and you square your shoulders trying to look bigger. Now your child stops bouncing and starts to cry. Loudly. You think, 'God the neighbours must hate us', closely followed by, 'This bedtime is going to take a long time and I still haven't had my own dinner'.

Rhinos are fierce-looking creatures with their huge bodies and thick skin worn like the armour on a Roman soldier. Ironically, a rhino is a super sensitive and misunderstood animal. Their skin is very sensitive, with the blood vessels on the surface of the skin, so they sunburn easily – not ideal if you live in Africa where the sun is hot and fierce. They have to wallow in mud as a form of sunscreen and moisturiser. Being very nearsighted means that a rhino startles easily, often charging at inanimate objects such as boulders or trees as they mistake them for a threat. To help them, they have developed a wonderful relationship with the oxpecker bird. This bird lives on the rhino, eating the tasty bugs off his sensitive skin, helping to keep it healthy. They also serve as an early warning system when there is danger. A rhino has to learn to listen to his friend the oxpecker to prevent him charging every rock or tree in an attempt to keep his family safe.

The rhino has gained itself the reputation of being bad tempered when in fact they are simply fierce-looking softies.

Oh, how some of us can rhino! And when we rhino this is precisely what we are like too. We are sensitive people who care very deeply about our families and our children. We only want what is best for them; we never intend to come across as the bully but sadly sometimes we do. At our best, a rhino has learned how to make use of body language, facial expressions and voice to hold boundaries in place so that a child feels safe knowing what they can do and when. We have control over how to use our body and voice to gain a sense of safety and control. We can use a firm voice and slightly cross face to convey a strong message to our child without frightening them.

At our worst, we charge at a behaviour or perceived threat at full speed without thinking it through or considering a different way of managing what is happening. We try to use control or coercion to force our children to act in the way we believe they should. It is often the 'do as I say right now or face the consequences' type of approach. If the child still doesn't obey, then we raise our voices, our faces look angry and we square our shoulders to make ourselves look bigger. In short, we try to intimidate them into doing what they have been told. If we still can't force them to stop doing what they shouldn't, then we charge! I can hear you muttering to yourself that nobody listens to you unless you shout. I hear you! We try not to shout in our house. If the kids aren't allowed to shout at me then I am not allowed to shout at them – remember the mirror neurons that teach my child? This 'no shouting' rule is harder for me than it is for anybody else! Not to raise my voice to try and gain some control means I must employ another way to be heard! Secretly, I want to shout precisely because it makes me feel better. Let's be honest with each other, shall we? I do feel better for a few seconds when I shout. In the car when somebody does something stupid in front of me, I will yell loudly and instantly feel a sense of power over them and yet, the truth is I have absolutely no ability to change their behaviour from the inside of my car, with my voice. I can scream and shout and let it all out (in the words of will.i.am) but it will not influence the other driver in any way, apart possibly in one. It is much more likely to trigger a negative reaction in them, causing them to yell through their window at me. My angry face seen through their window will trigger in the other person a negative emotion compelling them to try and feel safe. My rhino instinct to charge at the situation only causes them to charge right back. It does not cause them to stop and think about their driving so they can do better next time. Not helpful at all.

Emotions are contagious; the same parts of our brains light up. You shout, I shout. You slam the door, I slam the door. The mirror neurons are doing their job!

We rhino to gain control when we are beginning to feel out of control.

We use control to try and feel in control. Sometimes, we rhino because we are deeply afraid that we are about to jellyfish and that our emotions are going to take over. We rhino when we feel that nothing else works. Yes, you mutter again, if I don't shout and threaten then nobody listens!

Some of us were raised in the 'seen and not heard' years of parenting; I certainly was. As a young child, I never, ever said aloud the things I wanted to when my mother laid down the law! That would not have ended well for me. When my first daughter was born, I imagined that she would know the rules and obey them and as it turns out, she did not. Not only was she just a child who needed consistent boundaries, but she was also a child with sensory needs who found 'conventional' behaviour impossible. I remember a family member telling me that I simply needed to smack her more often to get her to comply. She was two years old. I ignored that advice.

We were all parented in one way or another, but we all made it to adulthood after all. I said in Chapter 1 that there are as many ways to parent as there are parents in the world. Your story and your experience are unique and therefore influence your parenting today in its very own way. Some of us had amazing parents, some of us had parents who made serious mistakes but tried hard, and some of us had parents who damaged us deeply. Then there is a group of us who had parents who were all three of those! How we were raised influences our own parenting, often in subconscious ways, and unless we take time to reflect on it, our past will continue to colour the way we raise our own children.

If you were raised in the era of 'do as I say and not as I do' then you may find it normal to shout to be heard. After all, what other way can you get a child to listen?

When I talk about rhino parenting in my groups, people often assume that I am suggesting we remove all boundaries and rules and simply get soft and complacent with our children, allowing them to take control of the family and reign over us like a 'mini me'. They assume this because we talk about no longer using shouting or fear to get a child to comply with their rules. This is absolutely the opposite of what I mean.

Knowing and teaching your unique family values is important. Setting boundaries and rules with consequences is essential to helping our children feel safe and secure and raising them to be happy members of society.

It is *how* we do this that matters. We must teach children right from wrong by modelling it to them. We don't need to shout it! We need to put boundaries and consequences in place without using fear to implement them. We can be both loving and hold a line.

Let us delve a little deeper in the rhino and unpick what the style looks like and what we can do to begin to make small changes. Small changes can have a ripple effect on our children's nervous systems and on our own, helping us all to learn a new way of connecting with each other.

Tone of voice

Our nervous system has an ancient memory stored within it that reacts with fight or flight to the sound of low frequency sounds. It reminds our bodies that when we hear the roar of a lion then we should probably run or get ready to defend ourselves. We are still wired that way; low sounds are a signal of danger. That is why when your toddler won't put on her shoes at Perfect Mum's house after a playdate, you smile (because Perfect Mum is watching) and you growl under your breath, 'Put these shoes on or you will never see the TV ever again.'

You deepen your voice in order to convey a little bit of a

threat to get those shoes on. The way we use our voices matters even more when we have a child who operates close to fight or flight as their natural neurological state, because when we are way out of our window of tolerance, our brain moves away from listening to the content of what is being said and focuses on the tone alone. High frequency sounds of a scream alert our brains to distress and have the same effect (Dana 2018).

This makes it particularly hard for men because their voices are already low. When they get frustrated, their voices may get lower and louder, easily causing a snowball effect in the child's brain. The child is in a stress pattern already, dad raises his voice the tiniest bit and boom, meltdown happens.

Even a mild, simple difference in the tone of someone's voice can change an interaction. Have you ever noticed how quickly your emotions can change when you are on the phone to someone? You can't see their facial expression or their body posture but you still feel what they feel. The first few words from the receptionist at the doctor's surgery can immediately tell you what mood she is in and change yours. The words spoken can be exactly the same, 'Good morning, doctor's surgery, how may I help you?' but convey different messages to your nervous system. For example, the promise of help and genuine concern when said in a sing song tone or the dread of no appointment or help when said in a monotone way. This can instantly evoke in you a similar emotion of either positivity or negativity.

Nicholas Christakis and James Fowler (2011) discuss this in their book *Connected*, which delves into how we influence each other. In an experiment to delve deeper into how emotions are contagious, subjects were placed in an MRI machine. They were played voices with no image conveying either a positive emotion such as triumph or a negative emotion such as disgust. The researchers found that the parts of the brain matching the facial expression linked to the tone of voice were activated. The angry voice activated the part of the brain that displays an angry face. The smiling voice activated the smile centre of the brain. Practically, this proves that an angry voice causes our brain to activate an angry facial expression, or an amused voice triggers a smile.

Our tone of voice alone can change how someone feels. Powerful stuff!

Learning how to keep your voice calm and even is a matter of practice. Try to ask somebody you trust if you tend to sound angry when you are feeling out of control. You know the moments I mean: getting those shoes on for school, asking your child to get off the PlayStation, telling them that they should stay in bed and not get out over and over again. Ask them if your voice matches the moment. The rhino has his friend the oxpecker who tells him when a threat is real or when he can relax and go about eating the grass without worrying. Who is your oxpecker friend? Who can you trust to help you know when you are looking and sounding angry at the wrong time?

I remember learning how to talk in a calm voice, often faking it to be honest. I would take a deep breath and talk in a calm, even voice and then my daughter would yell at me, 'Why are you using *that* voice? I hate it, stop!'

But eventually it became much less forced, less fake and I learned to manage my emotions with more success, so it was less confusing for her. My neuroception, my internal stress monitor, matched my voice (see Chapter 2 for more information). First, I had to understand that using a raised or deep voice to manage her just made it worse. I had to want to change and then I had to work on it. I asked my husband to be my oxpecker. I gave him permission to point out when I was being a rhino. This was not easy, and I often growled at him too. Over time, though, it helped me recognise when I was moving out of my window of tolerance. When I noticed, I could change my tone of voice and relax my body so I was less intimidating.

Practise talking in a calm and even tone of voice and see if it calms a situation down. Remember that we can build new neural pathways with practice, it is science. It does really work!

Facial expression

An adult or child who is in fight or flight already struggles to read facial expressions and often assumes everybody is angry. They can't naturally distinguish an angry face from a bored one (Dana 2018). Has your child ever asked you why you are angry when you are simply looking at your phone? This is a tough one for those of us with a face that does not hold much natural expression. My poor husband suffers with this! I often comment on his angry expression and he always replies, 'I am not angry at all, just bored or tired or thinking of work or zoned out...'

How do you know when a face is angry? The brow will be knotted above small eyes, your lips thinned out and pressed together or your mouth pulled up in a snarl. Your cheeks might be bunched up as you clench your teeth, and your nose will be flared. One way to be more aware of your facial expression is to pull an angry face in a mirror, take note of how it feels to knot your eyebrows, widen your eyes or make them smaller, purse your lips and flare your nose. Now, relax your face. See how different it looks and note how your face feels. What do the muscles around your eyes feel like? Is your jaw relaxed or tense? Is your mouth soft or are you pursing your lips? It is important to know what a relaxed face *feels* like in order to try and use it more.

→ **Try this**

How does your body tell you when you are stressed, angry, excited, happy? Think of where you hold strong emotion, for example your jaw, stomach, shoulders, hands. Do you clench your hands when you are frustrated? Do you clench your teeth together? Do you rock foot to foot when excited and waiting in line?

Body language

When we are in rhino mode, we can often make ourselves bigger by squaring our shoulders, lifting ourselves up a little more to tower over our child, stepping closer to the child and placing our face close to theirs. In other words, making ourselves look threatening. This is what we might do if we feel threatened by somebody we don't know too – we try to increase our size to intimidate the other person.

Remember where you hold your tension. Is it in your fists, your shoulders, your face? Take time when you are relaxed to notice what a calm body feels like. While you are not feeling stressed, how are you holding your shoulders, what are you doing with your hands or what do your muscles in your neck and back feel like? If we want to begin to change the messages our bodies are sending, we need to know what we are aiming to feel like. Then we will be ready to try a different body posture when we are next managing a difficult moment.

Something quick and easy for you to try is to consciously create distance between you and the child; step back or walk to the other side of a table or chair so it creates a barrier and prevents you from stepping too close. Sit down so you can't use your body to intimidate them, or crouch down to their level so you don't tower over them. Drop your shoulders while breathing out. Try to be conscious of what story your body is telling.

Do the opposite of what you feel

Next time you feel yourself want to charge in, take a deep breath, count to three and then do the opposite of what you instinctively want to do. If you wanted to shout, then whisper. Walk slowly, or slow your speech down. Drop your shoulders, take a step back from the child and relax your face.

Before you raise your voice, do something else first, for example walk to the toilet and back. Splash your face with cold water, take some deep breaths. Remind yourself that your loud voice, angry face and defensive body language will *not* make the situation better. You can still be in control, you can still set a boundary, you can still teach a child right from wrong without being a rhino.

Be patient with yourself

Changing a behaviour that has been imprinted into your brain is not quick, but it can be done. You may need to take time to reflect on why you feel so out of control and perhaps that might mean looking back into your own childhood.

Take small steps of change every day and acknowledge that you have done better. This could even be as simple as noticing you didn't react as quickly but stayed calmer for longer, or you didn't shout when you felt the overwhelming need to but instead spoke in a quieter voice. Each time you change the way you react, you are rewiring your brain and building a new neural pathway.

Think of a track in a road, or a path in the field at the end of winter. It is visible but not deep or clear. Each time someone walks the path, it becomes clearer and eventually, by the end of the summer, it is a deep and obvious path you can easily follow. This is what happens in our brains when we practise a new skill. We can build stronger, clearer pathways of a different way of reacting.

But we need to 1) Try to react differently, even just a little; 2) Notice when we have managed a small change; 3) Do it again and again and again.

One day you will think, 'Wow, I am reacting so differently from how I did six months ago.' It can be done; the science tells us our brains can learn and change.

Is someone else in your life the rhino?

You have read all of this and you may have recognised someone else in the words. We all need empathy and understanding about why we react in the way we do. And your rhino needs your understanding and love. What we do know is that it is much harder to feel empathy for someone who is angry and yelling. We don't first think about the trauma of their lives or the stress of their jobs causing them to move into fight. It is hard to feel empathy for a rhino. I am here to remind you that everybody deserves to be seen and understood. I am not saying that we should condone reactions that are frightening to others or cause upset. We should try to see the why under what we are seeing (see dolphin). If you are naturally more likely to be passive aggressive or a conflict avoider, you will find the rhino parenting style very uncomfortable. I often hear one parent accusing the other of being a rhino. When we reflect together, we uncover that one person is more of a jellyfish and is triggered by strong emotions. They are actively trying to avoid any negative emotions for fear or feeling out of control. When someone else in the family lays down a boundary in a way that feels tough or rigid, they don't like it. They may use words like, 'You are too hard on the children' or, 'You are too strict'. Perhaps their partner is some of those, but before you paint them with the brush of the hard-skinned, charging rhino, first check if your tolerance for any form of distress is low. What is your emotional state? Are you more of a jellyfish at the moment? When we are out of our window of tolerance then we find it much more difficult to manage a rhino.

Rhino in action

Back to our bedtime story. You tried using a calm voice, but it was just not enough because you were already too close to falling out of your own window of tolerance and your child could sense that. In the dolphin chapter we will explore why making sure you take care of yourself is not selfish, but vital, starting with making sure you eat something while you feed your child. When you notice your anger rising, try walking away from your bouncing child, splashing your face with cold water, and taking a few deep breaths before going back in. Drop your shoulders, notice your tone of voice, look in the mirror – are you looking as tried and fed up as you feel? Reflect on the story you are telling yourself. Are you anticipating failure before you have even started the night-time routine? Don't forget how attuned our kids are to us, so if you think it will all end in meltdown, you are telling the same story to your child without saying a word. How about imagining that there is another way this could go, that this could be an opportunity for you to try something new? Once you are feeling more in control, try slowing the situation down and connecting with your child. Use some breath games you both can play, for example blowing bubble volcanoes with straws in soapy water or blowing bubbles for each of you to pop. These sensory tools are not only good for calming both of your brains but also for helping lighten the mood and create connection. Now, once you are feeling calmer and your child is connecting with you, give them a clear expectation of what is expected: PJs, tooth brushing and bed. I know it sounds like a fantasy but it is science; if you calm down and connect with her, she will mirror your brain and over time you can build a new neural pathway for you both. It takes time and practice but it can be done.

★ *Chapter 10* ★

The Kangaroo

Nurturing and providing for our children's needs extraordinarily well, can be overprotective.

At its best, a kangaroo:

*   ★   knows exactly what their child needs to thrive
*   ★   is a brilliant advocate for their child and spends time educating others to create the spaces where their child can learn and experience life to the full.

At its worst, a kangaroo:

*   ★   overprotects their child and tries to keep them from experiencing any negative emotions
*   ★   feels that no one else can care for their child the way they do, so carries the burden alone
*   ★   puts in fewer boundaries with their child
*   ★   does things for them that they can do themselves.

I am sitting in a cafe on a rare trip with nobody other than myself to look after. Sadly, this is not a trip away to relax. I am here at a university far from home, to learn about sensory processing. These are still the days when you attend training face to face and not in the comfort of your own home. I notice the music in the cafe is loud and bouncy, the service is slow and it feels a little too hot. My immediate thought is that my daughter would not last very long in this cafe; this space would cause her to move out of her window of tolerance fast! I start to get up to find somewhere quieter to have a coffee when I remember that I don't have her here, so I settle back down in my seat. Being away from her is harder than I imagined it would be but not for the obvious reasons. I feel very differently about being away from her sister, way less worried, and she is three years younger! Deep down I feel guilty and fearful for leaving her because who can look after my sensory child like I can?

On the surface, my emotions make no sense; my husband and my mother-in-law are caring for her, not strangers. I have put in place lists, and acceptable meals are in the fridge, there are instructions and back-up plans, and my telephone is on all night for emergencies. Yet, even with all this planning I have had phone calls in the evenings, massive meltdowns with my daughter sobbing on the phone, begging me to come home. These phone calls are so upsetting for me, I have nearly thrown in the towel a few times and simply driven home in the middle of the night. I am considering this exact option as I sit drinking my coffee. The course can wait, can't it? My husband and my friends often tell me that I am overprotective and that I should let them help but they simply just don't understand what it is like. Besides, I have tried a few times and it always ends this way, her crying and me feeling totally overwhelmed with fear and guilt. This is my proof that she needs me, that I am truly the one person who understands her and can tailor life so that she stays inside her window of tolerance. That is why I am considering going home; although they love my daughter as much as I do, they simply don't know how to help her stay in her window of tolerance and I worry that the trauma will cause her damage.

Australians call a group of kangaroos a mob. As we talk through this parenting style you may agree this is an apt name for a group of kangaroos. Kangaroos are best known for the pouch females keep their joey (baby kangaroo) in. Joeys are born tiny, crawl into the pouch and stay snuggled there for ten months to grow strong enough to survive outside. A kangaroo mother will carry her baby around with her everywhere and protect it from harm while also protecting her joeys already hopping alongside her. Imagine a pregnant mother at the park with her toddler, keeping not only her family safe but also keeping an eye on everyone else. In a mob, kangaroos let each other know of impending danger by stomping their huge feet on the ground. They will box, kick or bite to protect themselves, their young and the rest of the mob. Beware a mama kangaroo, as she is fierce and protective.

The difference between a kangaroo bouncing across Australia and a human kangaroo parent is that the kangaroo knows when to let that little joey out of the pouch to join the mob. A kangaroo in the wild is not anxious about how its joey will survive, it is confident of what its young is able to do and how long it needs help for. It lets go more easily than we humans do. At our best, when we kangaroo, we know what our child needs to thrive. We ensure that they are surrounded by people who understand their needs by educating teachers, grandparents, aunts. We check that every environment they are in is set up to draw the very best out of them. We hold them close to us when they need us, nurture them and help them feel loved and safe.

When we kangaroo, we hold our little ones, and often our not so little ones, close to us to protect them from every possible negative experience or emotion. We try to keep them far away from places and people that might trigger them or push them out of their window of tolerance. We expend large amounts of energy ensuring that every space our child is in is totally safe for them from a sensory perspective. This can feel lonely and isolating because we feel that we are the only ones who know how to help our child. When we kangaroo, we demand less of our child or give them fewer boundaries to keep them calm and happy. Finally, the kangaroo feature I am most guilty of is that at times we simply do things for our children that they should be and are capable of doing because it is quicker and less dramatic than getting them to do it themselves.

Please don't mishear what I am trying to say! It is right and good for parents to keep their children safe, to help them when they struggle and to ensure that the environments they are in are not overwhelming or traumatic for them. Nurturing and keeping our children safe is one of our primary roles as parents. A kangaroo just forgets to check regularly if their child might be ready to try and manage more difficult situations.

We once visited a rescue centre for sea creatures on the Gulf Coast. We took a behind the scenes, personal tour around the facility and they showed us how they care for the sea turtles with injuries brought in from the ocean. They have blue ten-foot inflatable swimming pools filled with ocean water. Inside these big pools float smaller, colourful toddler pools filled with the same water. When the turtles arrive, they are frightened and ill, so they are placed inside the smaller baby pool and float around the top of the big pool. This way they only need to focus on their basic life functions in order to heal. When they are stronger, they are moved into the bigger pool and are monitored closely. More often than not they have to go back into the small pool for periods of time and then out into the bigger one. They go back and forth until they are ready to re-enter the ocean.

What struck me about this process is the time the staff take to monitor the turtles precisely to check if they can move on to bigger things. If they keep them in the wrong space for too long the turtle will deteriorate. The staff might be tempted to keep them in the smaller pools for too long because they are afraid they might not cope but this would prevent the turtle from learning to be the best it can be. Caring for the turtles always has the next step in mind, the next challenge, the next risk they have to take because their ultimate goal is for the turtle to be able to live away from the rescue centre and be free again.

This is exactly how we should parent our sensory kids, keeping the next big step in mind. When we kangaroo, we spend far too much of our energy working out ways to ensure that our child is never too distressed or that they can meet every sensory need instantly. We want to keep them inside their window of tolerance as much as we possibly can so we work hard at preventing any circumstance that might push them out.

Why might we kangaroo?

Tolerating the distress of our child can be harder for some of us than others. If you, like me, are easily pushed into jellyfish and become overwhelmed by your child's strong emotion, or into rhino to try and control it, you may be tempted to spend energy trying hard to keep your child regulated. You need them to be regulated because you get pushed out of your window of tolerance fast. This makes sense; feeling overwhelmed yourself is not a good place to be. We might be tempted to try and avoid any strong, negative emotions by ensuring that everything is always just right for our child. Our need to kangaroo may well be more about our difficulty tolerating distress than our child's ability to tolerate it.

Being finely attuned to the needs of our children helps us adapt ourselves and the environment to ensure they feel safe. This is a wonderful attribute, a parenting skill we could all strive to learn. However, when we kangaroo, we are at risk of believing that we are the sole person who can provide for the needs of our children. We unwittingly set ourselves up to the be the very best and we leave little room for others to learn too or do it differently. We may well have a small select group of chosen people that we feel can help, but we don't call on them too often. Of course, as we are exploring in this book, parenting a sensory child can't be always done in the typical way and does require us to educate others and help them to really grasp how to adapt themselves and the environment for our children. The risk when we kangaroo is that we hold it all close to our chest and forget to reflect on when our kids may be ready and able to tolerate another way of being helped. We risk expecting everybody to be like us.

Messages our western culture feed us through advertising and social media don't help either. Our innate, culturally culti-vated belief that 'being successful requires us to be happy' feeds our need to keep our children happy at all costs. We wonder if people look into our lives and decide how successful we are as parents by how our children are managing life. This is some-thing that I have had to reflect on, especially when my daugh-ter's mental health became poor and happiness was not always on the cards. As humans, we strive for comfort and happiness so that we can feel that our lives are a success. When asked what we want our children to be in the future, most of us will say, 'I just want them to be happy.' Yet, we all would agree that we can't always be happy all the time. Life is a rollercoaster; some moments we are simply just holding on. I love the Disney Pixar movie *Inside Out*. The emotions inside a young girl are depicted as characters, Joy, Sadness, Fear, Disgust and Anger. At first, we are all rooting for Joy to be the dominant emotion so that the young girl never feels sad or afraid. As the movie unfolds, we soon learn that she needs all the emotions. Sadness helps her feel joy. Fear keeps her safe and Anger fuels her to fight for what is right. It is all about balance. This is true for every human on earth. To be fully whole, we need to experience all of our emotions and know how to work through them.

We are also sold on the idea of knowing what is going to happen at any given moment and having control over all aspects of life. We want to know that we can control as many aspects of our life as possible and we dislike having to wait and see what will happen. Knowing feeds our sense of control. This translates to our need to have control over all aspects of life, including parenting. Not knowing how our child will cope with a situation or a person is exactly the opposite of this. We try to control as much as we can around our child so that we ourselves can feel more settled. Kangaroo!

As with all the styles we have discussed, our own experience of childhood influences how much we kangaroo our children. If your parents were absent and distant, you might want to be the opposite and be as involved as you can. If school was a hard place for you to be then you may assume school will not feel safe for your child either. It is true that often school can be a hard place for our sensory kids and that some teachers may need educating on how to help your child best access their skills. However, take time to reflect on how much of your own experience is colouring what you think now.

Finally, when we kangaroo, we often have not taken time to reflect on what our child is able to do now. Can he begin to tolerate moving out of his window of tolerance for a little bit so that you can teach him how to regulate? Are you still doing things for him that he really can do himself because you are just so used to doing it or you are anxious of what will happen if you don't? Are you avoiding places because you know your child will not manage them but now you are reading this you are wondering if you could in fact try again with a new set of tools and a different perspective?

Sometimes we have to let our children out of our pouch and out of the little pool to see what they have learned and how they might cope with new and challenging experiences. We can always step back in if they need more support. I worked with a boy who had just started secondary school. He was anxious; his sensory system found the transition tricky and it was not easy for him. His mother was brilliant at advocating for him and making sure he had all the support that he could get. She was so busy making sure he had every possible thing he needed that she had no time to reflect on what skills he was learning and how he was growing up. I asked him a few months into the new school year if he was walking to school with his friends yet or if his mother was still driving him. He said to me, 'I want to walk to school with my friends, but my mother is not ready yet.'

This is typical of us when we kangaroo. She was not ready to give him the space to try a new skill but he was. We worked together to help her overcome her fears, some of them valid and some not, and allow him the opportunity to try. Yes, it caused him stress but once he had achieved his goal of walking to school, he felt empowered and more confident of his ability to overcome the next 'hard thing'.

Remember that emotions are contagious and our children's brains are mirroring our actions. If you walk into a space expecting your child not to manage, you will be reacting without perhaps even being aware. Your child is learning from you about what and where is safe, often without you saying a word. When we are overprotective and anxiously attempting to make sure all is well around our child, we may be doing the very opposite. They are learning that places are not safe, that others can't help them manage or, worse still, they haven't got what it takes to cope.

Is your need to protect and ensure that your child is safe more to do with your own fear of what might happen if things go wrong than what your child would experience if it did? Things do go wrong, no matter how much you plan and prepare. Our children will never learn how to find ways to navigate life if we never give them the opportunity to try.

What can I do if I kangaroo?
Trust the science
Research tells us that safe, controlled amounts of stress can be beneficial for us. 'Good stress' helps motivate us and keep us focused, like the stress of preparing for a tricky meeting or getting ready for a first date. When we don't have high levels of chronic stress in our lives then a smaller amount of stress like falling over, losing at a game, or a small fight in the playground with a friend can be beneficial for us. Scientists have found that being exposed to these moments in life, and navigating through them with people who care for us, can help our brains build stronger connections and help us long term (Aschbacherab *et al.* 2013; Coan & Sbarra 2015). Did you do the still face experiment in Chapter 4? It was deeply uncomfortable for us not to be acknowledged or listened to but once the experiment stopped and we reconnected with the person, we felt better. The reconnection with the other person made us feel safe again. There was a repair of the short-term stress caused. If we did the experiment again, we would be better equipped to deal with our emotions because we have been through it before. The key factor here is the repair; without it we get stuck in a state of stress and trauma. Our children initially learn to regulate and feel safe with a trusted adult, not on their own. When they fall over, we cuddle them; when they are overwhelmed, we help them feel grounded. Eventually, they learn to deal with these events a little more independently. But they will not build the skill set they need to manage their sensory systems if they never experience anything negative. Acute, short-term stress

with a repair is good for us. How will your child learn to use sensory tools to help their body if you control every aspect of their day? You must gently help them find solutions. This is where you need to take time to reflect and find a trusted person who knows you and your child to talk with. It is all about constant reflection on what is best at what moment. When my daughter's anxiety was high, a friend told me that I was being overprotective because I chose to sit with her through her panic attack, meaning I had to leave the dinner table and miss a large part of their evening with us. I disagreed because I knew what my friend could not see, that my daughter was in full dissociation and she could not be pushed any further than where she was. I took in the whole picture of her day and her week and her overall presentation to make that choice. Months later, when she had learned a few ways to help herself and we had learned not to ride her wave of anxiety with her, the same statement from my friend would have been true. Then we were all ready to give my daughter the space to try and manage before I stepped in to fix it for her. It is up to us to take time to really think hard about where we are at and decide if the time is right to move them out of the small pool and allow them to feel a moment of acute stress so that they can learn to calm down.

We never learn how to get back into our window of tolerance if we never leave it.

Change your perception of stress

As we just said, not all negative experiences or emotions are detrimental to us. They give us the opportunity to learn to reframe what we are experiencing, use gratitude to get through them, learning that to be content and at peace does not mean to be happy and comfortable all the time. As adults, we know that getting all our needs met all the time is not the only way to feel good. To become resilient, we must learn to manage tough moments. We are the role models for our children. When we run ourselves into the ground keeping all negativity from them, they are watching and learning that all stress is bad and harmful. We are teaching them to fear adversity and problems instead of helping them view them as an opportunity to learn something new. When you change your perception of stress, you will learn that the hard moments can be a time to discover a new way, try a new tool and remind us of the good we have in our lives. Our children will learn this with us too.

Focus on the mundane moments, not just the highs and lows
Are you telling yourself the stories of the highs and lows of parenting? Do you remunerate what went badly wrong and wonder if you will ever have a good day again? As Kim John Payne says in his book, *Being at Your Best When Your Kids Are at Their Worst* (2019), we often focus on the highs and lows of parenting but focusing on just these two options limits our view of daily life. By doing so we don't notice the middle ground. Payne suggests something I have found to be valuable – we are always loving and emotionally holding our children, during the highs, lows but more importantly also during the everyday, mundane parts of life. They will feel our support and love all the time yet if we just look at the bad times, we can be in danger of losing sight of the fact we love them all the time. Sometimes they need us more, sometimes less, but we never let go of being there for them in between either. He suggests that these in-between moments are a great place to practise the skills you most need. Do you need to learn to give space for your child to be more independent? Practise letting her do more on her own when things are going smoothly. Do you need to practise slowing down and breathing before talking? Take time to practise when you are just getting on with the everyday things. Listen to your internal dialogue and if you are focused on the highs and lows then perhaps try to notice the in-between moments too.

Stop justifying your inner kangaroo
When my daughter was struggling at school, I was anxious every day she got on the school bus. Her emotions triggered mine and I was a complete jellyfish. We contacted the school

and they set plans in motion to help her, which did work to some extent. However, I hated feeling so out of control and anxious, and I felt better when I was involved in every part of her school day. I emailed, visited, called. I made demands for changes without giving the ones in place a chance to work. I became a kangaroo and I felt justified to be one. It took a discussion with a friend to begin to understand that my over-involvement was not helping, it was feeding my anxiety and in turn hers. Withdrawing a little, giving space for strategies to work or even fail had a surprising result. I anticipated a giant disaster that would cause irreparable damage. What happened was the opposite. Yes, many of the outcomes I was expecting did occur. She had meltdowns at school, she called me from the toilet cubicle in tears, I was called into school to collect her. Slowly, with consistent nurture at home, a therapist teaching her coping strategies, and the school trying to create an environment that provided for her needs, she began to find her inner voice. She learned how to ask for what she needed and she began to access strategies that helped her stay grounded. I gave her the space to experience adversity so she had a need to do it on her own. We knew she was ready to try. She is now a great advocate for her sensory needs, understanding that she needs to move more than others and she ensures that her work environment is set up to give her movement. She can tell her co-workers that they need to give her one instruction at a time and give her time before adding more. She builds in breaks to calm her nervous system when it gets too busy and loud. She needed me to stop making sure all was well so she could learn what to do when it was going wrong.

I encourage you to reflect on what moments you could allow your child to move out of their window of tolerance so they can begin to learn how to move back in.

Ask for help

This may feel hard to do, but allow others to take some of the burden from your shoulders. It can only be a good thing for someone else to learn how to help your child back into their window of tolerance, can't it? I know that for some of us, parenting is a lonely journey. I acknowledge that this is not a simple point. What I suggest is looking around at the friends, partners or other people in your community to try and identify if even one can be trusted to step into the field with you. Start small, not an entire night away but perhaps a playdate or ask them to help with a shopping trip or a play at the park. Take small steps towards allowing them into your world.

Kangaroo in action

I am sitting in the cafe and blame the distress my child is in on me not being home to care for her. The truth is that I am not seeing the whole picture in this moment. Helping me learn not to kangaroo is going to be a longer piece of work that requires me to consider how I am going to move forward from this moment. First, I need to reflect on why things are going so badly at home or more importantly, are they really going as badly as I think? In this moment, I am reacting like a jellyfish and the strong emotions my daughter conveys over the phone create in me strong emotions too. I am wobbled by her and want to get home to fix it. Reflecting on it with her years later, I realise that she did have moments of sadness, but she was safe, well cared for and was playing with her sister and watching her favourite TV programme most of the time. Was what I was feeling a real reflection of what was happening? She was not in as much distress as I was experiencing her to be. Her strong emotions and my inability to control anything from far away highlighted how much I was kangarooing. How could I prepare her and the family for the next time I had to leave for training? It was going to take some effort but it could be done. The planning had to include me allowing space for others to learn how to help my daughter without me controlling how it was done. I had to give them permission to help her in their own unique way. Another part of the process had to include me allowing my daughter to move out of her window of tolerance and to be confident she could learn to move back in without me.

I realise now with the benefit of hindsight that I had a low tolerance for her distress. I would instantly want to jump in and solve what was bothering her. While on the surface this is exactly the job of a parent, it has to be done in the way the people caring for turtles did it, with the bigger goal in mind. This would have helped me allow small amounts of distress and discomfort to help her build her confidence and skill set. Learning how not to kangaroo was about constant reflection and often being brave enough to ask others to step into my shoes at times, even when it didn't go the way I wanted. Keeping the long-term goal in mind helps you see the bigger picture.

★ *Chapter 11* ★

The Ostrich

Cares deeply for the family and looks after them well, can show too little emotion.

At its best, an ostrich:

- ★ is excellent at providing for their family and works hard to make sure they have all they need
- ★ always tries to give the very best they can with the information they have.

At its worst, an ostrich:

- ★ feels that their child's behaviours are exaggerated or facts have been distorted. They struggle to see the relevance of what is being pointed out to them
- ★ may avoid difficult moments at home by withdrawing, for example working long hours or hiding behind a device
- ★ excuses withdrawing from more challenging moments by saying they are providing for the family.

Noah is four and he has just been assessed by an occupational therapist. His parents are divorced, and he shares his time between them both. He has been brought to the assessment by his mother. Her main concerns are that he only eats a very restricted group of foods and gets overly distressed when she brushes his hair. She is also worried that he is always on the move and finds it impossible to sit still for any length of time apart from when he is playing with his Lego. Although she finds it hard to describe exactly, Noah's friends seem different to him when they come over to play. He is starting school later in the year and she is not sure he is ready. She talks at length about Noah's father who has labelled her as neurotic and disagrees that anything at all is going on. In fact, his main argument is that he was just the same as a child and he has turned out OK, hasn't he? She feels he is just not able to accept that Noah may need a little more help than other children. He did not stop her from bringing Noah for the assessment, but he refused to be involved. It is causing much tension between them as she is trying hard to get Noah's dad to recognise the signs of sensory processing difficulties, but he seems not to care at all.

The ostrich is an extremely powerful bird and the fastest animal on two legs. Ostriches are often depicted as sticking their head in the sand when things get tough. This is a myth – they would not be able to breathe, would they? The origin of this myth are nesting ostriches who are caring for their eggs. They dig a hole in the ground, bury their eggs and then regularly check on them by sticking their heads in the hole, gently turning the eggs with their beaks and making sure they are safe. From afar it looks as if their heads are buried in the sand. Although an ostrich is much more likely to face a threat head on, sometimes when a nesting ostrich feels threatened it may flop to the ground with its head and neck on the floor in an attempt to blend into the background and not be seen. It goes into a full fright state. This image makes me giggle as I picture an enormous bird on the floor of the Kalahari Desert, trying to look like a rock! Not the most effective way of avoiding danger considering how huge they are.

This is what we are like as parents when we ostrich; we flop to the ground and try to blend in. We attempt to make ourselves invisible and hide away from a problem that just feels too much to face head on. And the irony of it is that often those of us who are strongest find facing the harsh reality of a child who is struggling the hardest.

At our best, when we ostrich we are working hard for our family, making sure they are safe and cared for. Perhaps we are running fast, trying to make ends meet and yet we are acutely aware of the fact that we are being perceived as putting our head in the sand. In fact, *we* believe we are putting our head in the nesting hole and turning those eggs, making sure they are safe. Yet we are constantly being told to look up and stop hiding from the problem.

At our worst, when we ostrich we are ignoring the behaviours we are seeing or being told about. We feel that they are an exaggeration of the facts or a distortion of events. We hear our partner tell us about a possible diagnosis or about books they have read explaining why our child is struggling but it doesn't seem real to us. Often this is because we just don't know how to deal with it, we have no frame of reference to view it in or we simply don't want to see that there may be a problem at all. I remember a conversation with a mum at playgroup when my girls were little. Her son struggled, as my daughter did, with the loud, busy space and he would lash out at children. She told me the nursery called her to say that her child was biting other children. She said, 'I reckon the other kids always instigate it; he is a gentle boy at home. What exactly do they want me to do about it anyway? I am not there to keep his little teeth from biting a juicy arm, am I?'

This was a denial of the behaviour because she felt powerless to do anything to help stop it. She was still on a journey towards understanding that her son needed something more to help him stay in his window of tolerance, but she had no idea what. Denial and blame were easier. In her effort to make sense of what was happening, she had found a solution; the problem was the other children and her son was not to blame.

Sometimes when we ostrich we may try to avoid the difficulties at home by working long hours or filling up our time with other activities like endless hours of Netflix or staring at the phone, trying to keep our mind on something else so we don't have to face what is happening in the family. This makes sense when we still have not grasped that our child has needs that are different from the ones we understand. Sometimes we get stuck in the denial phase and aren't ready to face it all head on yet.

This can be a difficult place to be when there is one parent beginning to see and explore difficulties and another still sticking their head in the sand and pretending all is well with the world. Falling to the ground and trying to blend in until it all just goes away can take its toll on relationships.

If someone has given you this book and you are still thinking nothing is amiss with your child, then perhaps you are the ostrich? Don't put the book down yet; give it a chance. If you are at the start of your journey, be kind to yourself. Just by picking up this book you are already taking a step away from ostriching and looking up from the ground. For some of us, the process is similar to grief. In fact, at the risk of sounding too dramatic, accepting that your child is different is a grieving process. We have to look at the dreams we had for our family and we may need to adjust them. You are not alone in this. Give yourself time to digest things. Grief starts with denial where we are convinced it is not true. We blame others, we make excuses for why our child can't cope or we simply just ignore it all. As we begin to understand that something might be up, we get angry. This anger can be directed at our spouse, our parents, the system, the school or our child. Then we go into bargaining mode, trying to fix things. When we realise some things can't be fixed, we get sad. Eventually we accept the way it is and grow to love the new way our family looks. Most of us go around this loop over and over.

Where are you in this loop? Welcome, I am sorry you find yourself here. This is not the club any of us wanted to join. Be kind to yourself.

However, are you reading this chapter and thinking, 'Oh my word, my partner or my mother or my sister is such an ostrich'? They will just not listen to you and no matter how much you have been talking and giving them books to read, they are still not on the same page as you are. It feels frustrating and you are using any energy you have left trying to get them to see the issues from your point of view. They keep contradicting you and sometimes you wonder if it might just be easier to do it on your own!

What can you do?
Try to understand

This is a hard one. We all come at parenting with our own parenting past. We were all children once, every single one of us and we all had people raising us in one way or another. The way we were raised colours the way we parent our own children. This makes the way we approach the possibility that our child struggles different for each of us. Perhaps your partner is feeling some guilt for working long hours and deep down thinks it might be their fault. Or they view success as academia and being part of a sports team and so they feel a failure as a parent. Maybe they have never had to deal with a child that is atypical before and truly just have no skills to deal with him or her. This may be frightening and disempowering for them. Are you feeling resentful and angry so not reflecting on how tough this journey might be for your loved one? Try looking at it through their eyes and see if that helps you find compassion for them. They may need to start from a different point in the journey. If you are further along the path, give them time to catch up with you.

Give them a chance to try

Often we just end up doing it all ourselves because we fear the fallout if we don't. For example, you simply stop going out for a drink with friends in the evening because bedtime goes wrong when you are not there. You feel as if you have to do it all yourself. You may become resentful and isolated and never give your partner or the grandparents or sister the chance to try and find a way that works with their personality and your child's. I encourage you to give them the opportunity to try and manage some of what you carry. Yes, I know some will not want to take on the more challenging tasks like homework or bedtime but start where they are at. Find something they can do and give them the opportunity to build a connection that is unique to them.

Continue with your own journey

Sometimes we simply need to continue with our own journey of discovery and stop fretting about other people's journeys. If you are working out how to best help your child, simply carry on for now. Spending hours of your time and brain space working out how to drag your parent or sister or wife into enlightenment will burn you out. I am not saying give up and go it alone. I simply mean that fretting and getting frustrated is not likely to change somebody else's behaviour. Focus on you and what you need to learn. They may see how a different way is changing things and want to know more.

Build connection

This is especially for you if you are married or in a partnership. Being part of a team requires people to have a relationship. Parenting is tough and even tougher when your child is struggling. It is not possible to discuss calmly and reasonably how to deal with a child's challenging behaviour if you are not able to talk in general. Spend time together, reconnect. This does not have to mean a huge fanfare of babysitters, trying to get out of the house, and money spent on a restaurant. It can be a simple act of putting a candle on the table between the two of you while you eat the reheated spaghetti bolognaise or cold fish fingers after you have battled your child to sleep. Sitting down and making 15 minutes for your partner before crashing into bed can make all the difference. If you are blessed with help, then ask them to come and sit with your child on a Saturday afternoon while your child watches *Frozen* for the millionth time and you go for a coffee down the road. Half an hour is all you need. Make time for each other; remember why you fell in love in the first place. You will solve this parenting puzzle much more easily if you feel connected again.

Pull on your big girl/boy pants

Yes, you may be too mad at them. I hear you. You have been doing this alone. Your mother has let you down and told you that you should parent differently. Your spouse is never home. Your brother is judging you. Why should you make all the effort when they are not? Sorry, here is the hard advice I have for you: put on your big girl or boy pants and get over it. Sometimes we have to pull ourselves together and try again. Sometimes those relationships are worth fighting for and sometimes we must compromise. Sometimes we need to walk away and if you are in that place then there is no judgement. Walk away if that is what you need to do; I am not advocating staying in an unhealthy, damaging relationship.

You can do this

It is not easy trying to help other people see your child as you do. It is frustrating to feel that you are alone and judged. But you are stronger than you know. You are a warrior and you can do this!

I think I am the ostrich

It is often a slow process recognising that our child may not be neurotypical. Sometimes understanding feels a little like hide and seek; you just feel as if you can recognise that something is different and then it disappears again. It is helpful to start with wondering why you may be finding it hard to accept that your child may be neurodiverse. For some of us, it might be that the behaviour we see is a reflection of our own difficulties or we recognise our own childhood self in our child. We think, I was just like that and I turned out fine. This makes sense; much of what we have been discussing in terms of sensory processing runs through families. Accepting your child's differences may mean you need to accept your own too. Or you simply have no frame of reference in which to understand the behaviour you see, in which case, it is wonderful you have picked up this book to start learning some more and gaining that deeper under-standing. Knowledge helps us to view what we see through a new set of lenses and that can change the *why*. It can feel overwhelming when you see your child struggle so perhaps choose one aspect of what you are noticing and focus on that first. Learn about it and gain some skills. For example, start with understanding why they find certain fabrics impossible to wear and how you can help, or why they need structure more than your other children and how you can implement a routine. Be kind to yourself, take time to learn and remember that it is OK to go at your own pace.

Ostrich in action

Noah has had his assessment with the occupational therapist (OT) and she has recommended a block of therapy. The OT has suggested that Noah's father brings him in for the therapy every second week so that he can sit in the session and perhaps use the time to begin to understand Noah's sensory needs better. During the sessions, he confides in the OT that he avoids brushing Noah's hair when he stays over and only does it when it is time to go back to his mother. He says he finds the screaming too much. This is a good starting place for him to begin to explore one small aspect of Noah's sensory needs. The OT suggests he asks his best friend if his son also gets overly distressed with any form of grooming. He tells her the next week that his friend's son does not get as upset and he is wondering if perhaps it is something he needs to learn about. He is beginning to see the behaviour through a new lens, but it will take time and patience. Noah's mum continues her journey of finding ways to help Noah, slowly introducing techniques that work to his dad, for example playing deep pressure games before hair brushing. He reports back that the games seem to help with the distress, but they take up far too much time in the morning when he is in a rush. He is on his own journey in finding what works in his space with Noah. It is a slow process; Noah's parents have to communicate and learn together. She has to give him time to catch up with her as she forges ahead with building the puzzle that is Noah. There are no easy answers, and they will move forward and back many times. We will need to change our view of Noah's father; he looks after him well and loves him deeply, but he is his own unique person. He may need more compassion than Noah's mother feels he deserves as he works through the process of accepting the sensory needs of his son.

Chapter 12

The St Bernard

Calm and compassionate, holds boundaries consistently.

At its best, a St Bernard:

★ is compassionate and has taken time to learn more about what makes life a struggle for their child

★ is learning how to remain calm even when they don't feel it

★ sets boundaries and is consistent in holding them

★ chooses the battles to fight carefully

★ can hold a boundary without using shame

★ often remembers the 'good stuff' in themselves and their child.

As soon as one tiny ray of light peeks through the curtain, Jen's eyes pop open. Sunrise is at 5am today! As her feet hit the floor, her energy levels are at 100 per cent and it feels to you as though they stay there until her eyes reluctantly close way after bedtime. After a messy, half-eaten breakfast it is time to brush Jen's teeth and tame her bedhead hair. You were already beginning to feel stressed about the hair brushing while making breakfast. It isn't just the hair you are thinking of, to be honest, it is the socks and school uniform in general. And shoes! It is the whole morning routine that makes you anxious; Jen finds it all so hard and makes it known loudly. Recently, the neighbour has come out to ask if everything is OK as you leave for school. To make it all feel even more stressful, Jen's older brother gets really stressed about being late for school, and you are all late most mornings because Jen simply will not put on those socks!

The St Bernard is iconic for its search and rescue capabilities. But before these large dogs showed their aptitude for finding people buried under the snow, they were used to guard pilgrims as they passed through the Great St Bernard Mountain Pass between Italy and Switzerland. A notoriously dangerous pass, the dogs would guide pilgrims through and guard them against being attacked by thieves. When Bernard de Menthon opened a hospice for weary travellers, the dogs were part of the deal. Here Bernard found they were brilliant at finding people trapped under the snow and rescuing them. They carried with them the iconic barrel; some say it contained whiskey, some rum and others believe it held a homemade, regional concoction perfect for helping very ill people survive (Kas 2019). The St Bernard has a reputation for being gentle, compassionate and sacrificial. However, we must not forget they are also dogs bred to guard their humans, so they are strong willed, loyal and willing to stand up to behaviours that are a threat to those they love.

When we are a St Bernard, we are able to climb up that snowy mountain to find our child, connect with them where they are at and coax them, frozen solid and reluctant, down that slope back to safety. A St Bernard is consistent, slow to anger, quick to forgive, calm and rich in love, even when the situation is very emotional. He does not panic or shout, which may cause an avalanche. Rather, he tries to be warm and nurturing while providing strong, clear boundaries. The St Bernard is the three Cs: compassionate, calm and consistent.

No, no, I hear you! This is so easy to put down on paper and feels so very hard to actually do in the heat of the moment. The challenge is this: we are often much better at telling ourselves what we have done badly and very seldom look at what we are doing well. Remember the yellow cars earlier in the book? As you read the rest of this chapter, try to find the moments when you are already compassionate, calm and consistent, even the little, nearly invisible moments. They are there if you look for them!

We are often much better at parenting than we give ourselves credit for.

Let us take this one concept at a time. If you see a heading that grabs you, start there. Nobody can work on everything at once, but we can make small, steady changes that move us forward. We can absolutely learn to react differently; we can learn to change our responses. Our brains have the most incredible ability to learn new reactions with time, repetition and allowing ourselves to try. If I can do it then you can too!

We need to be patient with ourselves and take time after a meltdown to reflect on what worked and what didn't. We need to press the reset button in our bodies often during the day, forgiving ourselves and starting again. When we make a conscious choice to change just one little way we react to any part of life, it can have a ripple effect.

If you want the same outcome then you must continue to do the same thing. The converse is obvious: if you want a new outcome then you must change something. When a couple dances a waltz, if the person leading changes the direction of their shoulders alone, the couple changes direction. It is a subtle move with a large change. Our brains are connected to each other. A small change has the same effect and can change the direction of a relationship.

Let's have a look at what can help you be a St Bernard.

Compassion

I was watching a TV programme where a newly appointed housing officer and someone from pest control were inspecting an empty property. Opening a kitchen cupboard, they found it filled with cockroach poop, lots of it! The camera panned in on the face of the housing officer who was retching. She looked up at the camera and said something like: 'Next time somebody calls to say they have cockroaches, I will be kinder to them. I never knew this is what it can get like!'

Knowledge and understanding gives us compassion and it changes how we react to others. Understanding creates in us a desire to make it better for that person.

It is so hard sometimes to feel compassion for a child who is screaming, throwing things or simply will. not. sit. still! There are times when your child is genuinely making life hard for you and now, I am asking you to have compassion.

The reason we spent time in the first chapters examining the science of sensory processing and our brain was to deepen our understanding of what drives our children to react in the way they do. It helps us know when they are unable to control the way they behave and when we need to give them our compassion. Looking at the brain may even have helped us understand why we find some aspects of life difficult ourselves.

We often confuse having compassion for someone with giving them the freedom to do whatever they want. We wonder if having a deeper understanding of what drives their behaviour means we won't put a boundary in place. In fact, this is the exact opposite of what compassion is.

For example, my husband finds Christmas with any of our extended family really stressful. He gets quickly overwhelmed in loud and busy places. Understanding his sensory overload and how his brain goes directly into fight mode does not excuse the fact he yells at us to be quiet when we all talk over each other, getting louder and louder. Having compassion for his overloaded brain and increased cortisol levels helps me understand that the loud, crazy lunch that makes my heart fill with joy makes him feel overwhelmed. Compassion stops me from telling him that he is rude and needs to grow up. It helps me work with him to try and find a way for him to feel more grounded and understood. It is still not OK for him to shout but I react differently to his needs. I can hold a boundary with love and compassion. It does not change the fact he shouldn't shout; it simply changes how I approach him.

(In the interest of honesty, every Christmas I lose compassion and so every year I make him feel bad for his overload. I don't get it right all the time either!)

Be calm and slow to anger

Never in the history of all arguments has someone calmed down when the other person said 'calm down'. I am not simply saying, 'calm yourself down!' Staying calm when chaos is reigning around you is a skill, a skill that can be learned. Yes, it can! First, let us take time to reflect on how you react to the huge emotions your child experiences. Do you jellyfish and become quickly unsettled? Do you step right into rhino and try to take control so that you can feel in control? Or do you retreat emotionally like our friend the ostrich? The first step is to reflect on your immediate reaction to the emotions or sensory overload of your child. You move out of your window of tolerance and your brain takes over leading the charge, either taking you into fight (rhino), fear (jellyfish) or freeze (ostrich). Let us think back to what we learned in Chapter 2 about our brain. Dan Siegel gave us a visual way of remembering by using your hand. Tuck your thumb into the palm of your hand and make a fist (Siegel & Bryson 2011). Your fingers represent the upstairs brain, your cortex (thinking brain). Your thumb and wrist are your downstairs brain (limbic system) where fight, fight and freeze are activated. Now, keep your thumb tucked in but lift your fingers up. If downstairs (your limbic system) is fully active, your thinking brain (your cortex) disconnects so it is hard to solve problems, reflect, understand the situation well.

Here are a few tips for staying calm:

★ Stop and breathe deeply before talking. With practice, you can learn to use a few seconds to stop, breathe and calm down. Deep breathing slows your heart rate and calms your downstairs brain. It is science! Breathing is a fast, easy way of changing what is happening in your brain (Dana 2018). Practise deep breathing when you are calm; don't wait until a war is going on in the kitchen over chicken nuggets. Try breathing deeply when you get in the shower, lie down in bed at night, while driving or at any moment when you have a few seconds to be intentional about your breath.

★ Talk it out. I use my husband as a sounding board. I start with, 'I just need to tell you what I feel but I don't need any answers or help.' I vent for a few seconds and then put my big girl pants back on and step back into the arena. Talk it out with a friend, a therapist, your sibling.

★ Fake it until you make it. Acting calm when you are experiencing a huge emotion has two wonderful side effects. First, it changes the dance pattern you and your child usually engage in. They are used to you reacting a particular way when they overload. When you don't, it will change the way they feel and react. Second, you are beginning to teach your body that you can stay grounded and calm when faced with an overwhelming emotion. And you can build a neural pathway that uses that pattern more easily next time. Fake it until you make it!

➜ **Try this:**

✓ **Stop** – don't be impulsive, take a deep breath, wait before you react.

✓ **Tune in** – become aware of your self-talk, emotions and body signals.

✓ **Act** – once you are calm, try to problem solve.

IT'S OK TO FAKE IT UNTIL YOU MAKE IT!

Practise talking in a calm voice – talk into the mirror, check your facial expressions, ask your partner or friends if you 'look' and 'sound' calm.

Be consistent

I remember my three-year-old daughter asking me over and over for something I had said no to over and over. Exasperated, I eventually asked her why she kept asking if I had clearly said no. She looked me in the eye and said, 'Because if I ask again and again, sometimes you say yes.'

Rumbled by a three-year-old! Sometimes we are just too tired or fed up with the constant battles, the meltdowns, the sensory seeking and constant movement, the loud voice even when you have asked for a little quiet or the refusal to eat the pasta they loved yesterday because 'today it smells funny'. And so, we compromise, and we choose to move a boundary, just this one time so we can have a break from it all.

It is harder to keep boundaries in place than to let them slide. That is why sometimes we just don't do what we know we should. It is also harder when all of the people who love your child aren't on the same page. One of you is soft and the other strict. The result is a child who knows they can get what they want by asking over and over! Choose your boundaries and hold them firmly.

Choose your battles

We have made our lives more complicated than they need to be. Keep your life as simple as you can. We are so easily drawn into this crazy concept of what our families ought to be. All around us we have images and concepts of what a perfect family should look like. Advertising, television and, even more powerful, the uber mum at the school gate with her organic, sugar-free cupcakes! All this pressure that the world places on us is covertly hidden behind what often looks like a 'good thing'.

Not all good things are things we need for ourselves or our family. A St Bernard can look around their family and choose to let go of things. You take time to re-evaluate what is part of your DNA as a family, what you want your children to take into their own families one day. Keeping our lives simple helps us to remember what our ultimate goal as a family is. Maybe you don't need to fight every battle. Choose one at a time and hold that boundary consistently. If this week you are choosing food as your battlefield then perhaps you can let go of putting shoes on. If you decide you want to get your teen to go to school every day then maybe you need to let go of something else. This way

you are not trying to fight everything, and it stops the tempta-
tion to let go of a boundary because you feel overwhelmed by
constant fights. Choose your battle and be consistent with it.

Set boundaries without shame

Be quick to let go of what has caused your strong emotions.
When we hold on to our anger or pain, our disappointment or
irritation, then we may be tempted to use them to try and hold
a boundary in place. And that opens the door to shame. When
my daughter was in junior school, she was a master at masking
her anxiety during school but when I came to collect her, she
would often unravel. I *felt* that the other mothers would judge
me about my parenting. Truly, I doubt they even noticed; this
feeling of judgement was rooted in my own view of my parenting. Yellow cars again!

I was always on the lookout for what was going wrong and
so I saw it. I felt a failure as a parent, I felt judged and was angry
with my daughter for making me feel this way. One afternoon
when she ran off angry into the woods near the school, the first
thing I said to her when I reached her was, 'You have made the
whole school look at us and wonder what is wrong with our
family.' I used *my* emotion to shame her into behaving differently next time.

I needed to take time to reflect on my part in what was
going on. She had had a tricky day and was in flight mode. I,
on the other hand, was worried about what people thought of
me. What I was bringing to the table was not hers to carry. It
was my part to deal with.

Take time to reflect on what is happening in your heart.
What is *your* stuff to work through and what is your child's
responsibility? When we take time to reflect on our strong
emotions during the trickier moments, in can help prevent us
from placing responsibility for our emotional needs onto our
child. This in turn will stop us from trying to shame a child
into changing.

Be rich in love and nurturing

Remind yourself what you love about your child. They are uniquely created; they are entirely awesome. Take time to get to know them again through the lens you are beginning to build for them. Their unique take on life and love is part of who they are. Make time for them again, time to be together doing something you both enjoy, even if it is only for a few minutes. Try to nurture them in the way they receive love. You are their safe space and they want to be with you, even the teenagers! All children want love and time from their parents.

Remember when you did things well

Practise remembering when you did a better job during a meltdown. Remember the moments that have gone well. Focus on these; recreate them for yourself so that you change your internal narrative from a place of not being able to help your child to a knowledge that you do have skills that can help. This takes time and giving yourself permission to notice and talk about what you have done well.

Listen to your internal dialogue

We are so good at telling other people how marvellous they are, but we spend so much time reminding ourselves of what we are doing wrong. How you think of yourself matters because it fuels how you react to triggering moments. An elite gymnast can't walk out onto the floor to do a routine when she is convinced she is rubbish and will fail. She will injure herself that way. She must have a large amount of self-belief and confidence in her skill set even while she is aware that she may make mistakes. She has to learn to trust the training she has done. We are allowed to and should think on what we are doing well as parents and not get stuck on what we are lacking. If we go into the day thinking we are a failure then we will end up injured.

St Bernard in action

There is no magic wand to make this morning routine run the way you would prefer. Jen wakes at a reasonable time, she doesn't jump on the sofa as soon as she is downstairs, she sits at the table and eats a full, fruit-filled breakfast after which she brushes her own teeth and hair, puts on her uniform and waits with her book bag and PE kit by the front door for her brother to get ready. Her shoes are on, her coat is zipped shut and her water bottle is tucked into her bag. This is not realistic, even for those parents who have children with no sensory needs!

Let's use a few of the tools we have learned together to think through this morning routine, and remember we are not looking for solutions that change everything. We want small changes in the right direction and to be willing to go back to the start a few times before we find solutions that work. The St Bernard is all about compassion, learning about how Jen's brain processes sensory input and how she feels when she is outside her window of tolerance. Part 1 of the book will help you have a deeper understanding of who Jen is. Compassion is the building block for connection and as we have said many times, connection is the first place we find safety as humans.

What is the goal we are trying to achieve on a school morning? This is the best place to start, as we can't work on everything at once. We can, however, choose one aspect and start there. For example, is finishing all the food more important than how or where it is being eaten? Are you working on Jen getting dressed independently and are not too worried about getting that uniform on or is the goal simply to get those socks on no matter who does it? If we know what one aspect we want to focus on then we will feel less overwhelmed by trying to fix it all. Once you have chosen what you want to insist on, then try to be consistent with that boundary. We are often tempted to change the boundary to make a moment easier because we have moved outside our own window of tolerance. Reflect on how you hold a boundary and where.

The St Bernard tries to stay calm but this can be even more tricky when Jen's brother hates being late. Is his stress level making yours rise too? Could a friend come to help take him to school so he is on time and you can focus on Jen? Maybe it is time to ask for help with the morning routine and asking someone to take him to school may be a simpler place to start. This may also help you stay calmer and more able to connect with Jen. Let us not forget what your sensory system needs to stay calm. Planning ahead and having some strategies for Jen can help but you may need to build in a few activities for your own nervous system. What would you need to stay in your window of tolerance? What about getting up a few minutes before the kids so you have time alone, or making sure you have your favourite coffee in the house? Small things can have a big impact on our brains.

Adding some sensory tools into the morning routine could help Jen feel grounded and may also help you feel more in control too. Jen is sensory seeking and needs much more movement than other children to register sensory input. What we also might find good to know is that Jen has already worked out what she needs to get ready for the day – she needs to move. If she was an adult, she may be the person who gets up early to go to the gym or has a run before work. Her body needs movement (vestibular) and heavy muscle work (proprioception) to feel grounded. This might be hard for us as parents when we are easily overwhelmed by all the sensory seeking so early in the morning. Your instinct might be to try and convince her to sit still. Perhaps you could change your perspective on the movement, have compassion for her and create some spaces where she can get this movement safely and easily, without overwhelming you? What about a small trampoline in her room, some big bean bags for her to jump and crash onto? Perhaps she could have a peanut therapy ball to sit and bounce on if she is allowed morning TV programmes? Think of your space and what you already have at home and purposefully create ways for her to move.

Add more crunchy or chewy foods to breakfast and a curly straw to drink from; try some sugar-free gum while putting on those socks. The gum could also be an occasional replacement for that toothbrush! Remember your oral motor system is powerful!

Now those dreaded socks! First, have you looked for seamless, softer socks? Many clothing shops and supermarkets now stock socks and school uniform that has been designed for our sensory kids. They are softer, have fewer seams and no labels. Don't forget that deep pressure overrides most uncomfortable tactile input. Try some deep pressure before the socks go on, rub Jen's feet, give her some deep hugs, maybe get her to sit with a weighted toy on her lap while those socks go on.

The St Bernard tries to stay calm, compassionate and consistent. This is easy to write and not always easy to do but remember, our brains are excellent at learning new ways of functioning. You have had many moments of excellent parenting, so remember those when things are hard.

Chapter 13

The Dolphin

Curious, connected and playful.

At its best, a dolphin:

★ is curious to look beyond behaviour to find the underlying cause of what they are seeing
★ is playful and makes time for activities that bring shared joy with their child
★ learns how to look after themselves so they can stay regulated
★ regularly reflects on their child's skills and state so that they know when their child is ready for more
★ learns how to connect with their child on their level
★ celebrates themselves when they have done well.

Our parenting group sits in a circle with fresh coffee steaming in mugs, cupcakes on plates ready to be eaten. A mother tells us she is anxious and desperate for answers. Her son is heading into his teen years, the hoody has been purchased and he hides himself in the hood as per the stereotype; this she was expecting. What she was not prepared for was the change in his sensory needs. When he was younger, they had created a pretty well-oiled machine of sensory tools to help him manage his days. In particular, she told us, he had always struggled with coming back from school feeling overwhelmed by the day. At the start of the sensory journey, school would tell them that nothing was wrong, and he was managing well there but when he got home his emotions would be huge as he tumbled way out of his window of tolerance. There were many meetings with therapists where they implemented a variety of tools to help him navigate school, including a sensory diet of regular sensory strategies throughout his day to help him feel regulated. Now, he has moved to senior school and while the first year seemed to be going well, he has become sullen and withdrawn. He comes home from school, drops his bag by the front door and simply flops on the sofa. He stays there until dinner time without engaging with his family. He simply seems to shut down and tune out to the world. In fact, she has been on the internet and she is concerned he is depressed. Gone is her son who needed to bounce for an hour on the trampoline after school.

As we sit with coffee mugs in our hands, we listen and begin to ask questions. What have you tried? She says she has reminded him that he has always loved to move and how good it was for his brain. She has encouraged him to jump on the trampoline and even go for a cycle around the block. She has tried using positive reinforcement like more TV time for each ten minutes of physical activity and then resorted to the consequence of less time if he didn't. Nothing is working. He has no interest in what he enjoyed before. She has called the school but they say all is well there and they are not concerned. The group groans; this is the standard answer, they all agree, and it does not mean school is going as it should be. In the group, we try to find something concrete she could do in the next week to help her feel less anxious, so she doesn't move into jellyfish or kangaroo. We think perhaps she could spend some time wondering with him about what he feels he needs instead of suggesting what she thinks might work. What activities did he enjoy now he was becoming a teen? Could she find one he would like to do with her? With this, we put down our coffee cups and head off into our busy, sensory-filled lives.

Dolphins are intelligent and sociable creatures who live in family units called pods. Just like us humans, they enjoy moving between homes and pods to visit each other. Dolphins love to be social. There is growing evidence that they may even have names for each other (Dell'Amore 2013). The image of a dolphin calling out the name of another across a coral reef makes me smile. Their young stay by their side for six years before becoming independent and, just like primates, dolphins can teach each other skills. They can demonstrate and learn from other dolphins, teaching each other how to use tools to get to food or where the best fishing spots are. They are also problem solvers, with many reports of dolphins working together to find solutions; they are great team players.

Dolphins look out for each other; they learn from one another and they play together. They are joyful and curious, quick to learn, and love to chat with each other.

When we dolphin, we swim gently alongside our children, making sure they know we are present and available. We tell them they are loved, and we spend time on activities that bring shared joy. When we dolphin, we learn to help ourselves stay regulated so that we can help our children regulate. At our best, we have taken time to understand our own areas of need, where we are vulnerable and easily triggered. This helps us to anticipate moments when we will not manage as well and gives us time to put in place some strategies to help ourselves. As dolphins, we regularly reflect on our children's skills and state. This enables us to know when they are ready to move out of their window of tolerance, so we can encourage and guide them through the process. A dolphin is there to catch them if they fall out of their window too fast, and stays calm and regulated when they feel overwhelmed. A dolphin is about curiosity, connection and guidance.

Be curious

A dolphin can dive deep under objects in the ocean to investigate what is underneath. When we dolphin, we try to be curious about what is underlying the surface behaviour we are seeing. This can help change our internal dialogue about why our child is struggling. Looking back at Part 1, we spent time thinking about some of the possible underlying causes for what our children are experiencing. Sometimes the anger or anxiety, the inability to focus, the constant movement, refusing to do homework, hiding away from us are not a choice but our child's brain trying to find a way to feel safe and regulated.

Another word for being curious is to mentalise. This is when we make sense of each other's emotions by reflecting on *what* we are feeling and *why* we might be feeling that way instead of simply reacting. When we take time to dive in under the surface behaviour, we often find the reasons driving what we see. We might even find out why *we* are reacting the way we are and what is triggering us.

I have often made assumptions about what my daughter was feeling in a particular moment. Being curious was a revelation because most times my assumption was wrong. I might have seen her bouncing about the house, sensory seeking and finding it hard to sit still. My first thought would be that her energy levels were high and she needed to go for a skate to burn some energy off. Being curious and asking what she was feeling often revealed high anxiety or frustration at the root of the continual movement. Knowing helped us connect to address the anxiety as well as using a sensory strategy like going for a skate.

Our nervous systems are unique to each of us. Mine is not like yours and yours is not like your child's. We all need a different experience to bring us back into a calm state when we are out of our windows of tolerance (Dana 2019). Be curious about what your own and your child's nervous systems need to come back into connection with each other. What does your body need to come back into social engagement? Is it the same or different to what your child needs?

With an older child, you could do it together. In a calm moment when you are connecting, talk about it, reflect on what your body needs to feel regulated and ask them what they find helpful. Often, what we think they need is not what they think they need. It is fascinating in the clinic when a child and a parent talk about what their bodies need. As therapist and parents, we are often surprised by what the child thinks works, and it is sometimes very different from what we thought it should be. One young boy who found it hard to sit still and do his homework told us that he would get much more done if his mother let him move around the room and not sit at the table. An agreement was made to experiment in the week to see if this would work or not. Mum and I were sceptical. To our surprise, he got all his homework done in record time that week but he wasn't sitting at the table. He came over and wrote the answers down one at a time as he ran from one end of the room to the other. Being curious with him helped his family find a solution that worked for his body.

In our home, waiting until the storm had passed, we would reflect with our daughter about what would help the next time she was outside her window of tolerance. She needed to get on her bike and ride in the fresh air for half an hour. For me, it was a deep pressure hug from my husband, listening to some music and breathing deeply while she was out on the bike ride. The next time her anxiety started rising and we noticed it, we encouraged her to go and ride her bike while I took a moment to calm myself too.

When we teach our children how to pay attention to and understand what they are experiencing we are modelling to them how to view their emotions in light of their sensory needs. Our end goal is for our children to be able to be curious about their own emotions and what their bodies need to feel safe so that they can connect with those they love. Let's face it, when we are overwhelmed, angry or anxious, we are not able to build relationships with people. In order to connect with people, we need to feel regulated and grounded.

Ask questions

Dan Siegel (Siegel & Bryson 2011) gives us some wonderful tips on how to talk with our children in his book *The Whole-Brain Child*. He suggests that we should first acknowledge the big emotions they are feeling through our body language, facial expression and tone of voice and, if we must, then our words. Remember that we are not able to use our cortex, our thinking brain, when we are in fight, flight or fear. He also notes that we must try not to judge. Once the situation has calmed down, you are feeling more grounded, your child is feeling less over-whelmed then you might ask a few questions. Be curious about the behaviour with the child, trying not to narrate. By narrating I mean telling them the answer you think fits the problem. For example, when your child gets upset because screen time is over, you could say, 'You were cross because I didn't give you more time on the iPad.' True, they might well be cross because of this but it could be something else too. You can help them reflect with you about what is happening. 'I wonder why you felt so cross?' 'Let's wonder what is going on in each other's mind.' 'What's happening? Could it be this or that?' 'When did you start feeling like this?' 'Let's try to work out what was happening together. I was feeling this. What were you feeling?' This will create a space for your child to identify what they are feeling and why. You may be surprised by their answers. As I said, when we assume, we know we can get it very wrong.

Important note! It is not possible for you to be curious, calm and able to think about what is happening when you are not feeling safe and grounded!

Look after yourself and your relationships

All the neuroscience tells us that it is much more difficult for us to create that safe space of curiosity and calm when we our-selves are not regulated (Dana 2018). Think again about how our brains are connected to each other and how we can influence another person's emotions through our own. If your own neu-rological system is in a state of fight, flight or fear then you will be more easily triggered by your child. If you are tired, hungry and stretched for time then the constant bouncing on the sofa or the inability to wear a school uniform that has not been tumble dried will push you quickly out of your own window of tolerance. When you are not feeling emotionally regulated then you will find it much harder to help your child navigate their own strong emotions. Mirror neurons. We feed off each other's state.

→ **Try this**

Reset your nervous system by:

- ✓ slowing everything down: your breathing, your speech, how fast you are moving
- ✓ splashing your face with ice cold water
- ✓ taking a break in your 'simmer down space'
- ✓ putting your favourite song on at full volume
- ✓ taking a walk around the block or a drive in the car
- ✓ running up and down the stairs a few times, stomping your feet as hard as you can
- ✓ noticing five things you can see around you, four things you can hear, three things you can feel, two things you can smell and what you can taste.

Sometimes I get half-way through my day as an occupational therapist before I notice that every child has been pushing boundaries, refusing to engage with me or literally bouncing off the walls. For most of the day I will have been thinking, is there something in the water today? Is it the weather? Is the space too hot or cold? Why is every single child having a bad day?

It often takes me a long time to wonder if the common denominator in the day is me! Hard as this might be to admit, it is often me having a bad day, not the children! I am what is changing the atmosphere in the room. It might be a day I am overtired or worried about something else. It might be that I am still annoyed at everyone at home for not packing the dishwasher but leaving the plates right next to it and not *in it*! My dysregulated state changes the dynamic in the room. With every single child!

How we feel and where our nervous system is at matters! I am therefore telling you that you *must* do the activities that calm you down, make you happy and grounded. Need to spend time with a friend? Have you had that massage you have been talking about for a long time? When did you last go for a walk alone so you could notice the nature around you? Do you need to go for a cycle ride or a drive? Go to the gym?

Finding and doing what is good for you is nearly more important than anything else when you are parenting.

OK, so your life does not allow space for some of what you need. There have been times when I could not leave my daughter to go and do my own self-care. It is not always possible to do what you would like. Parenting a child with sensory needs sometimes means you can't go out or, if you could, you might simply not have the energy to.

Here are a few creative ways of doing self-care when you can't access what you really want to do:

★ Time-out chair for yourself. I had a chair in the corner of the room that I would go to sit in, mostly only for a few minutes or even seconds before I was needed again. I chose this chair to be the place I would calm down. I put some magazines and colouring books and pens next to it. I would simply sit down and breathe, just for a short time. It was a conscious choice to sit and calm my nervous system there. Soon my brain built a new neural pathway that allowed me to calm enough to carry on. It was a short-term, quick solution for the moments that get too overwhelming. The bathroom can be a great space for this too.

★ Music can be a fantastic way to help regulate. Take time to make a playlist of songs that either create in you a calm feeling or give you energy. Music has been proven to be able to change your state (Dana 2018).

★ Nature can be healing. Plan a walk or a trip to a forest or your local park or green space. Notice the way you feel when you are surrounded by the open space or by the trees, the sounds around you, the air, the feel of the tree bark, the leaves. Research tells us that nature taps into the calming parts of our brain and can help bring us out of fight, flight or fear (Twohig-Bennett &

Jones 2018; Slavin, Pemrick & West 2022). Maybe think of bringing home a rock or leaf or stick to put next to your time-out chair. This can serve as a reminder of the way you feel when outside and help your brain to remember what it feels like to be calmer and more grounded.

★ Date night with your partner or a friend (see the Ostrich chapter). Can't go out? Babysitter too complicated to arrange? There have been many evenings when my husband and I have made spaghetti bolognaise into a date night meal. Add a candle to the table and bring out the posh mugs for the tea. Invite a friend around to watch a movie with you, make popcorn and allow yourself time to relax. Use connection with others to feed your soul.

Share joy with your child

Most of what we have to do as a parent involves some goal or other, doesn't it? Bedtime stories can be about teaching our child to love books and read. Bake together to teach life skills and maths. Get them to school, help them with homework, get shoes and socks on their feet, keep them clean, and on and on. Sharing joy is about creating moments where there is no agenda apart from having fun. What do you feel when someone you love makes time for you? Real time without the phone and not 'quickly checking emails', time where you are the sole focus? It is lovely, isn't it? I encourage you to find some activities with your child in your week that are simply joyful and fun. It may mean you have to step into your child's world and play their game. A young person I was seeing recently came into a session bursting with stories of how he and his father had built a village on Minecraft together. The young man could not stop talking about how his father had told him that every Monday evening he would make sure he was free to play online with him, no matter if he was in the office or at home. What a simple idea that created in the young man a sense of being seen and loved. Sometimes we forget that the simple act of playing a song and dancing in the kitchen can be enough to fill the space with joy. Joy and laughter are strong antidotes to fear and anxiety!

Find a pod of people who understand

The most powerful part of the group parenting sessions we run is not the information we share about the brain and parenting styles. What helps nearly every parent sitting around the coffee table most is being with others who understand what it feels like to parent a child with sensory needs. There is no judgement as we share our fears, our own angry outbursts and our disappointments. We can relate with stories of family members who continue to ostrich or give advice we have not asked for. Finding a place where you can talk and be understood is life-giving. Find somewhere you feel heard and supported. For me, my church family is it. I know they care and will be there for me when I need them. No judgement, just love. Who is in your pod?

Celebrate yourself

We spent a little time in St Bernard talking about changing the way we think about ourselves but this time I want us to think of celebration. This is more than simply noticing when we are doing well, this is about throwing a little party in our hearts for ourselves. Wait, I hear you say, isn't that a little self-indulgent? I don't think so. How many times have you celebrated the things your child has done, small or big? We cheer when they pee in a potty or when they get their exam results later in life. Why not afford the same joy to yourself?

In the Kangaroo chapter, I spoke of the rescue centre on the Gulf Coast. While we were there, we watched a dolphin show. A storm was brewing in the distance, the thunder was rolling towards us, but the dolphin, the star of the show, was not perturbed. He would listen to the instruction the handler gave, dive down deep into the pool and then come flying out of the water, twisting and leaping with joy in a great show of how well he was doing. We all clapped and cheered; what a clever animal! That was when the handler quietly told us that in fact, the dolphin was not doing what he was asking at all. He was simply celebrating himself, loving the applause. He wasn't really doing all that was needed but he was still pleased with himself for trying.

We should all be more like him. He wasn't doing exactly what was expected from him but he knew he was good enough. He knew he was doing enough to deserve our applause. And what you are doing right now is enough. You are doing the best you can with what you have. Celebrate yourself, give yourself some credit. Maybe you can reward yourself with something you love to do; it may even become something you can do without thinking too much about it.

Dolphin in action

Let's go back to our mum sitting in our group, wondering about what might be going on with her son. His mood seems to have changed and the sensory tools she has used in the past seem not to be working. This change is wobbling her, causing her to feel a little like a jellyfish as she becomes more anxious and is perhaps being pushed into kangaroo, as she wants to overprotect her son. A dolphin spends time being curious and wondering what is behind the behaviour we see. The mother has already started this process, has she not? She knows her son's behaviour has changed; she is trying to work out the *why* so she can uncover what he needs to feel seen and supported. Being part of the group is a good place to start, as talking through concerns with like-minded people, some of whom may be further along the road and know a little more, is often eye-opening. Remember the research we saw in the Rhino chapter that showed that when someone we know does something well, we are statistically more likely to do well too? This mother can learn from the others in her group. For example, one parent tells us about the brain changes that happen in adolescence and how our sensory needs change alongside this. Often the sensory strategies that worked for our child no longer work as we move into the teen years and we need to start our detective work again. Our teens need to take some ownership of looking after their needs, even just a small amount at first. We also encourage her to go home and be curious. She reports back to us that he seems grateful that she has taken the time to ask him how he feels and listen to his response. She has wondered with him about what is going on at school to cause this change and what they might be able to do together to implement a change in that environment. He doesn't confide much to her about the school day but she feels it is time to call a meeting with his teacher and investigate it further. What she learns is that his body is shutting down after school and he really feels he needs the time on the sofa to unwind and feel grounded. They agree that she will bring him a snack and his weighted blanket and leave him alone for an hour. In return, she suggests they do something together when he has rested. They are still working on the details together, but she feels much more positive and the group can feel the change in her anxiety. Being a dolphin has not fixed the situation completely, but it has helped the mother and the boy reconnect at his level and at his pace, creating a space where they can begin to work on what they both need to feel safe again.

★ *Part 3* ★

SENSORY STRATEGIES AND MAKING A PLAN

★ *Chapter 14* ★

Planning for Success and Planning for Failure

The school fair is tomorrow, and experience has taught you that this afternoon of candyfloss, visits from the local fire department to show off their fire trucks and the general chaos of sugar-filled children can become 'the best day ever' or a complete disaster. You have no control over how loudly the announcements are made over the sound system, you have no idea what sudden schedule changes will be made to the programme and so you can't prepare your child for it at all. You enter the whole afternoon with an underlying sense of dread which is enhanced by the memory of a meltdown at the last fair that was so epic the school secretary still talks about it at her knitting club.

As you get ready for the fair, drive over and walk through the school gate, your child is reading your body language. He has not forgotten the last meltdown either and is also wondering if he is going to get through the day without another story for the secretary to tell.

Why even try to plan for an event that you have little control over and where the outcome feels inevitable?

Planning for success and, more importantly, planning for failure, equips us as parents to feel more in control and less anxious. As we have discovered repeatedly in this book, your state has a direct impact on your child; your brains are connected. Feeling more in control is a better place to start than a state of high anxiety. While you are getting ready for the fair, you are already telling your child the story of your state without saying a word. They are watching you and their brain is making a move towards calm or towards anxiety. They are reading your story and changing their inner narrative to match yours.

What do I mean by planning for failure? Let's look at a simple concept I teach parents to use. We start with plan A, B and C.

Plan A is when all your preparation works. Your child arrives at the fair well regulated after you have given them a good meal that they actually ate; they have had a sensory break on the trampoline, and they have their favourite t-shirt on to show their teacher. During the fair, you notice them becoming dysregulated by the fire truck's sudden siren and you get them outside for a sensory break just in time. The day runs smoothly, candyfloss is consumed, the fire truck is explored and it is indeed the 'best day ever'!

Plan B is a variation of plan A. Perhaps the favourite t-shirt is not clean but you have found an acceptable alternative, albeit after some negotiation. The food you carefully prepared is no longer acceptable but you convince them to eat something else in the car on the way there. You don't notice the unexpected siren because at the exact moment it goes off, you are in the school office being held hostage by the secretary as she tells an endless story you are too polite to interrupt. When you eventually come out of the office, you find your child crying and hiding behind the candyfloss machine. All is not lost though as you whip out the ear defenders and a lollipop for them to suck on. The day feels scratchy and hard, but you get through to the end of it with some success. It is not the 'best day ever' but a version of it, a 'good enough' day.

Plan C is the disaster scenario. Nothing goes to plan; your child moves out of their window of tolerance half an hour into the fair and starts screaming. You leave through the school gate with them flailing in your arms. You glance up as you leave and see the school secretary watching from the office window. Oh, she can't wait to see the knitting club girls on Tuesday to add this little scene to her ongoing story of your family.

Why am I asking you to plan the disaster scenario? Well, it is a simple brain technique. If you have planned for it then it is less of a shock and not entirely unexpected. You are ready for it; it is not a disaster after all but it was part of your planning. You feel less of a failure if you have anticipated things not working. Please note, this is *not* the same as spending all your energy catastrophising and over-thinking every detail. We do not want to move into jellyfish or kangaroo. It is an opportunity to briefly consider what could happen so that it settles you enough to change the story your body is telling.

If you do end up living Plan C, spend time later over a glass of wine or cup of tea reflecting what caused Plan C to evolve instead of Plan B or A. Think of what you can do differently next time, if anything at all. Sometimes Plan C is just what it is, and we need to move on. More importantly, think of what did go right; there are always some moments, even in the midst of a disaster that have gone well, for example you actually managed to leave the house to go to the fair even if you left in a blaze of tears. Sometimes, Plan C is an opportunity to learn or discover another piece of the puzzle that is your child. It is not a failure, it is a moment for feedback.

Here are some areas to consider when planning. Some may be more important for your child than others. Some may not be relevant to you and your family at all. Use the ones you feel will help you and ignore the rest.

What is the goal you are trying to achieve?

When our daughter had meltdowns that involved throwing chairs, my husband and I initially found it hard to work together in the heat of the moment to help her. Sitting one evening it dawned on us that the main reason we could not work together was that we had totally different ideas of what we were trying to achieve when the chairs went flying across the room. I wanted to keep our daughter and ourselves safe. I was not concerned about the consequences of the chairs flying in that moment; I could not be bothered by them breaking. I struggled not to become a jellyfish and ride her wave of emotion with her. I was working hard at trying to find a way to manage myself and think of how to help her. My husband, on the other hand, was focused on disciplining her, helping her to see how dangerous her behaviour was and making the consequences clear to her. This was his way of trying to bring some control into a situation that felt frightening and dangerous. He was a rhino. Once we agreed on the outcome, we could work together to help her. We realised that we needed to connect with her so that she felt safe and able to be calm; we needed to give her space and walk away if necessary, but make sure she knew we were on her side and not against her. Setting the boundaries and consequences for broken chairs came later, when we were all calm, and this had to be done without shame or anger. We had to work out what it was we wanted in the moment. Going back to the fair, you plan around what you feel the outcome should be. Is it a teachable moment for your child to practise managing a busy place? Or do you want them to see friends and feel included? Would it be enough for them to show their t-shirt to their teacher and climb onto the fire truck for a few minutes? What would make you feel that this outing was a success, even if you hit Plan B or even Plan C?

The environment

Think of the space you are going to be in. How loud is it going to be, how busy? Is there a place you can retreat to with your child or a place for them to access the movement they need to regulate, or will you be confined to a small area? The environment outside your home is rarely something you can change but you can consider how to use the space to create what your child needs. For example, putting in a little thought about where a quiet corner would be at the fair so you can remove yourself from the crowd prevents you from having to look for a space just after the siren has gone off. Planning spaces you can use ahead of time can give you a sense of control and lessen your anxiety. Thinking about the space may also prompt you to pack other items into your bag, such as ear defenders, something to do in the quieter space like a fidget toy or a favourite book, or maybe a snack you know he will like.

Unavoidable roadblocks

Some things in life can't be prevented and have to happen. We need to eat and drink to stay alive, we need a safe place to live in and we need people to care for us and nurture us. Other parts of life might be considered to be unavoidable, like having to see a doctor, going to school and brushing your teeth. What we are in danger of doing is seeing the roadblock and feeling defeated by it. We can also allow our fear of the consequence to stop us from considering an alternative. The truth is that most things can be changed if needed, but we sometimes need permission to think outside the box. Getting your child to keep their teeth clean is important but there are many ways to achieve the same goal. There are chewable toothbrushes, for example. Or even more crazy, perhaps you could leave tooth-brushing for a few days and focus on another battle that has a higher priority. Not every battle needs to be fought. In our family, attending school felt like a part of life that was not negotiable, especially when my daughter began secondary school. It caused great anxiety in me when she became so anxious and overwhelmed that she could not even get out of bed to go. Much of that lay in my fear of what it would mean for her if she didn't attend every day. Would she end up with no education at all? Would we get into trouble with the local authority if we let her attendance drop? Life changed when I was able to change my perspective. Thinking of school as something we could at times let go of (with all the right permissions in place of course), so that we could focus on her mental health instead, shifted a huge weight off my shoulders. This in turn changed the dynamic around school and eventually she was able to go in more easily. Not all roadblocks are unavoidable; many of them can be tweaked to help us guide our children through and learn new skills. Allow yourself to first, think outside the box, and second, change your perspective about which battle is most important at this moment.

Other people

Who else is involved and are they helping or hindering? When you are planning, think of who else is going to be around. If you usually struggle with getting those socks and shoes on at home, it is not going to be any easier when you are visiting your mother-in-law. In fact, depending on your particular mother-in-law, it might well be more stressful if she helpfully gives advice and opinions from the sofa. Planning for this might mean that while you are visiting, you don't insist your child put on their shoes independently or you might simply resort to bare feet or crocs when going out. It also gives you the opportunity to talk it through with your child so that they know who is going to be there and why things may be a little different that day so that you don't have to try and explain in the moment.

Language

Think about the language you are using. Are you giving too many instructions at once? Mornings are a pitfall for this. We issue instructions one after the other: fetch your lunchbox, put it in your bag, you have PE today so don't forget your kit, have you got your water bottle, why are you wearing the dirty jumper again and not the clean one I left on the bed? On mornings like this, we may turn around and look for our child, only to find they are building a Lego tower in the living room because they could not process all the language coming their way. We need to be aware of what language we are using, especially when we are feeling stressed and close to the edge of our window of tolerance. Often one word at a time is enough when you are all moving out of your window of tolerance.

Parenting style

Reflecting on what style you default to when situations get stressful helps when planning. Are you more of a jellyfish when you are feeling stressed? Or a rhino? How is this impacting the situation and how can you help yourself stay more in control? A jellyfish at the school fair would find their child hiding behind the candyfloss machine and immediately feel overwhelmed with guilt for leaving them while also desperately trying not to feel their child's sadness. A kangaroo might walk over to the fireman and give them a lecture about loud, unexpected sounds and ask them not to do it again, despite the fact that the other children enjoyed it. And a rhino might grab the child by the arm and pull them out from behind that candyfloss machine and directly out of the door into the car while scowling at the fireman as they pass them. What is your default? Plan around it. Do you need to ask a friend to be on standby to come alongside you if things get tough? Do you have to go to the fair alone or can your sister come along as a second pair of eyes, ears and hands? Do you need to make sure you have regular sensory breaks too? Knowing your default parenting style can help you in your planning.

Triggers

What are the triggers that cause you and your child to leave your window of tolerance? This is as straightforward as it seems, but we often forget to think about our triggers when we plan something. Thinking about your outing to the fair, an obvious trigger point might be the sudden loud sound of the siren. To be honest, with all the other things we have to think about to get ready, we may not take it into account. Having recognised this as a possibility, you could either get your child to wear their noise-cancelling headphones or you could have a quiet word with the fireman and ask when they are planning on doing the demonstration. Armed with a little notice, you can decide what is best to do. Planning will give you the head space to remember your child's auditory processing difficulties. What are your own triggers? Mine would absolutely be the school secretary. When I feel judged and watched as a parent of a sensory child (which happens way more than it should), my window of tolerance shrinks dramatically and I become a wobbling jellyfish or intimidating rhino. Neither work well for helping me and my daughter navigate situations. Being aware of my trigger point, I might find subtle ways of avoiding the secretary or ask a friend to save me if she sees me being cornered. Triggers are so obvious that we often forget to plan for them.

Making a plan

As parents of a sensory child, we often take all of the above into account without even being aware of it. We have a mental checklist we zoom through before we leave the house. Who has time for more? Not many of us to be honest! I encourage you to take a little of the time you can find between all the other things you are doing to take one situation your child struggles in and to unpick it. What do you want to achieve in the situation, what factors could be playing a role: the environment, people, triggers, language, roadblocks and anything else you think of? I am confident something will be highlighted to you that you have not considered. This is a simple tool to help you feel more prepared for what life might throw your way as you navigate the world side by side with your sensory child.

Let us think about building a sensory tool kit next. When we are making our Plan A, B and C it is helpful to think about the sensory tools we can use. We will first think about the why and then the how.

Chapter 15

Building a Sensory Tool Kit

Building a sensory tool kit is not an exact science and can sometimes feel a little frustrating. We find something that works brilliantly for a little while and then, seemingly overnight, it stops working. Or even more annoyingly, we try a multitude of sensory activities, and we just don't see the changes we are hoping for. The danger is that we decide that all this 'sensory stuff' is in fact just rubbish and we stop trying.

Finding what works for you and for your child is an ongoing piece of detective work. You, together with the professionals supporting you, look for pieces of the puzzle and slowly build a picture that makes sense. Sensory processing is always part of a bigger picture and so will never be the answer for all the issues you are facing. We use sensory tools in conjunction with other things that work for our child. A sensory tool is any activity using our eight sensory systems to access our lower brain, helping you to reconnect your cortex to your limbic system, so that you can reason, think, focus or make sense of your emotions. A sensory tool could be something you already do every day, like taking a walk at lunchtime to reset your brain for working through the afternoon, chewing on strong, minty gum to help you finish that essay, or having a long, cool shower to relax. Sensory tools can also be very intentionally added to your or your child's day to help them manage what is expected, for example regular movement-rich breaks throughout the school day or using a fidget toy during carpet time.

We established in Part 1 that our brains are not static and set in stone but can learn, change and are connected to each other. We know that what we see on the surface is not always the whole picture. We have to take time to look at all the elements that are at play when we are trying to find solutions that help.

Why does sensory input work?

The *cortex* is responsible for higher-level functions such as planning and problem solving, making sense of our emotions by reflecting on them, thinking things through before simply reacting, and so much more. It is where our executive functioning happens and is what Dr Siegel calls the upstairs brain (Siegel & Bryson 2011). Our upstairs brain is completely reliant on the lower levels of the brain to be working well. If downstairs is having a party, then upstairs can't concentrate on what it needs to do and it disconnects. When you leave your window of tolerance you are not able to think clearly or process information like you usually do. Go back to Part 1 if you need a reminder.

The *limbic system* triggers the release of adrenaline and cortisol causing your body to protect itself by going into fight, flight or freeze mode. When the limbic system is working well then it also helps you focus and attend, keeping your body and brain in harmony so that you can be your best self.

The *cerebellum* takes in proprioceptive and vestibular information from your body and feeds it into the limbic system. Here it can either up-regulate you or down-regulate you. Up-regulation is using your body to 'wake your brain up'. For example, you might have to write a report for work, but you are tired and unable to concentrate after a long day of sitting at your desk. What helps you 'wake up' so you can get the report done? You might get up from your desk, stretch out your limbs, walk to the kitchen and make a caffeinated drink. Better still, you could go outside and walk around the block in the fresh air to the coffee shop for that hit of caffeine. When you come to sit back down, your brain seems a little more 'awake'. Your cortex was struggling to think, plan and process so you used your body to send information through your cerebellum to your limbic system by moving and activating your muscles. Here it wakes your brain up just enough for you to reconnect your cortex for a while longer.

Down-regulation is calming your brain and body so that your cortex can re-engage. For example, you have had an argument with a colleague at work. You get yourself so upset that you are not able to find the words to convey what you mean. What could help you to think through a response that is both clever and well delivered? You could take yourself out of the situation and go for a walk around the block to the same coffee shop you visited to wake your brain up. The same input through the movement and muscle activation will feed through your cerebellum to your limbic system and calm you down.

Seeing how the areas of our brains work together helps us understand why using sensory input can change our arousal states and help us move back into our window of tolerance.

We are looking for small changes

When our child is struggling and we are finding it exhausting, we want something that will make the situation change quickly and completely. The world we live in has a quick-fix for many problems: if you have a headache, you can take a tablet; if you order a book online, it can be delivered the same day; if you are hungry, you can pop a meal in the microwave without much effort on your part. The truth is that there are no quick-fixes for a sensory child who struggles; it is a slow process with many elements to consider. When we put in place sensory tools, we are looking for small changes, perhaps even only a 1 per cent improvement. Each time we find something that works a little, this is a move in the right direction. Small, steady progress is what we are looking for.

What works today may not work tomorrow

In Part 1 we explored some of what can affect our brains, for example how much sleep we have had or the levels of stress in our lives. How we process sensory input is not static; it is reliant on many elements. That is why one day we love loud music and the next we need the radio off. If you have tried a sensory tool and it worked for a while and then stopped, keep it in the back of your mind. It may well work again at a later point.

Be intentional about using sensory tools

Be clear about what sensory activity you are doing and why, so you and your child learn what helps you to feel more in control of your bodies. Be curious and notice what is happening. Remember that we find evidence of what we are thinking about. Yellow cars and pregnant ladies. Being intentional can really focus us in on the small, positive changes a sensory tool can make. For example, when you notice your child finding it tricky to sit still at the dinner table, you can point it out without shaming them and offer a solution. 'I can see that your body needs to move because you are finding it tricky to sit still and eat. Shall we see if we can find something to help your body feel more ready? What about running up the stairs and fetching my water bottle?' Then when he comes back, you can note any changes you see, 'I notice that you seem a little more ready to sit now. Running up and down the stairs really seemed to help.' Or, 'Are these socks making your feet feel fizzy? Shall we see if they feel less fizzy after I give them a rub?'

For an older child, you might note how you have noticed their anxiety become slightly more manageable when they use their ear defenders during a shopping trip or that doing homework after a skate around the block is much more effective. Remember, we are looking for a tiny change, not a magic wand! It helps our brains slowly build a new neural pathway when we notice the changes and keep trying.

Take part in the sensory activity with your child

Some activities can be done together and create a moment of connection. You may also find that your own nervous system calms, and sensory tools are not just for our children after all. Co-regulation is how your child first learns how to feel calm; remember Chapter 4? Your baby cries, you lift them up and hold them close, rocking your body slowly side to side. They begin to calm down and so do you. You regulate together. It is just the same for sensory tools. Using deep pressure, for example, can be something you share. You can play a deep pressure game and gently squash them under some pillows to help calm, and then they get a turn to squash you under the pillows. Take a walk together or ride your bike around the block with them. Practise taking deep breaths together or blowing a feather to each other. We all use sensory tools to regulate, and you might find some that work for you too!

Having access to tools can help you feel less anxious

Planning for and having access to different sensory tools might not always mean you can stop a meltdown from happening. What it can do, though, is help you feel more in control and prepared. This small change in your own state has a direct impact on your child. Carrying a crunchy snack in your bag can help you stay a little more grounded when your child starts to leave their window of tolerance because you know from experience that a tiny shift in their nervous system can have a big impact. It is helpful to carry with you sensory items that help you and your child when you go out; for example, if the spare set of ear defenders are in your bag then you will feel less worried about a party getting too loud. Have access to fidget toys or oral motor tools. Just a few items can help you feel more in control.

Sensory tools are part of a bigger picture. They can be powerful but they can never be offered in isolation. To be effective, sensory tools need to be offered with curiosity, compassion and connection. We need to take time often to reflect regularly on what is working and what needs tweaking. Experimenting with sensory activities with your child can be a fun way of creating connection and relationship too.

Let us look at some sensory strategies next, thinking of what *we* need to feel calm and in control, as well as our children.

Chapter 16

Sensory Tools

Using Your Body to Regulate

Building a tool kit of sensory activities is a process that takes time. Sadly, there is no formula you can use to discover what will work and when to use it. The very best way to find what sensory activities will work for you and for your child is to see an occupational therapist who specialises in sensory processing. Having a professional assess your child is the most effective way to determine what exactly is going on and what will help. What we see on the surface is rarely the full picture, and an in-depth assessment may uncover things you have not noticed before. I would encourage you to consider using a variety of professionals in your journey as part of finding out what puzzle pieces fit where. The right occupational therapist is well worth investing some time and money into.

Sensory activities are best used as part of your daily routine. You may have heard of a sensory diet. The concept of a diet is a wonderful way of viewing sensory input. Sensory diets are like eating food and drinking liquid. You are better off eating and drinking regularly throughout the day instead of waiting until you are so hungry you feel unwell or so thirsty you have a head-ache. Sensory input is best added throughout your whole day so it becomes part of your life. You may find that you already have many sensory tools in your day. This is a great place to start, thinking about what works already and then building on that.

Let us take a quick look at some of the sensory systems and what you can implement. This is not an exhaustive list of activities, and your occupational therapist, books and some fantastic groups on social media will give you more ideas.

Please note, it is very important to stop anything that causes your child discomfort or appears to make them more dysregu-lated. Never carry on if your child is asking you to stop or they are showing signs of distress such as nausea, sweating, flushed or red cheeks, becoming tearful or pulling away from you. All activities must be positive and fun. If they are not, then stop.

Oral motor tools

Our oral motor system is one of the most powerful tools to help us feel calm and grounded; we are wired to use our mouth to regulate from birth. A baby feels safe and relaxed by sucking on a bottle or their mother's breast. As we grow up, we continue to use our mouth to regulate. How often have you stopped what you are doing to get a cup of tea or coffee to help you either wake up your body or feel calm when you are upset? Next time you are in a long, boring meeting have a look around and notice how many people are chewing on their pen or finger to try and stay awake.

Ask any mother of a sensory child, and you will find that they always have a snack of some sort in their bag! You may not know the exact reason why, but you do know that when emotions are beginning to wobble, the offer of a snack can change the mood.

A mother described to me how she always took a bag of crunchy carrots or crackers to her son's boy scout meetings. Waiting to go in with the hustle and bustle outside the door would cause him to move out of his window of tolerance and that would prevent him from going in. She found that giving him a crunchy snack to eat while waiting helped just enough to get him through the door. The crunchy, chewy food served him in the way a pacifier would have as a baby. If you think of it that way, you can see that drinking a smoothie through a straw or sucking on a water bottle could have done the same thing.

Calming tools and activities include sucking sugar-free lolli-pops or a sports water bottle, curly straws, juice boxes with a straw, warm drinks such as hot chocolate, subtle flavours like cinnamon, blowing, for example using a straw to blow a cotton ball across the table, blowing bubbles.

Alerting tools include crunchy and chewy foods such as popcorn, carrots or apples, dried fruits, raisins, nuts, crackers or fruit and nut bars, cold drinks such as icy water; strong flavours such as mint, citrus and spice.

30 seconds to experience

What food groups or drinks do you reach for when you are feeling tired or upset? Is it the texture you like, the taste or the combination? All of us use our mouth to regulate, often without thinking about it. How are you using yours daily when you need to change your mood?

Breathing

Using your breath is a quick and powerful way to access your lower brain and bring you back into your window of tolerance. Just keeping your breath in a rhythm whether it is a shallow in and out or a deep filling of the lungs can help you calm down. Trying to get your breath out of a ragged, anxious pattern into a rhythm can be very powerful (Dana 2018). Often children hate being told to breathe when they are feeling overwhelmed; I can't tell you how many times I have been told, 'I hate breathing!' Teaching our children to use their breath can be fun but remember to practise when they are feeling calm. If we only ever ask someone to focus on their breath when they are already struggling, we cause them to associate it with something negative. Try to encourage conscious breathing all the time as a way of life, and this will be really helpful for you too!

Start with the practice of drawing in a deep breath and blowing it out slowly. You can do this with pinwheels, blowing bubbles, straws in soapy water to blow bubble mountains, blowing bubbles in your milk with a straw, blowing up balloons or keeping a feather up in the air with your breath. Cara Koscinski's (2018) book, *Interoception: How I Feel* will provide you with some simple, effective ideas on teaching breathing as a form of regulation.

Once you have mastered drawing in a deep breath and then slowly letting it out, you can add in breathing visuals. These are tools to help you keep that rhythm going such as drawing a finger over the outline of your other hand and breathing in when you are going up a finger, holding at the top and then breathing out as you trace down the finger. Move all the way around the hand. Figure of 8 breathing is similar; draw out a simple 8 on paper, trace your finger around and breathe in on the first circle, hold in the middle and breathe out on the second circle. If you have no paper then trace the 8 in the air or the palm of your hand. There are many ideas on the internet to give you a visual tool.

Introduce taking a deep breath in and out all through the day. We like to do this in our therapy sessions; for example when the child is trying to plan an obstacle course we might say, 'Stop, take a breath and think about what to add next' or, 'Before you jump off that block, take a breath in and out to get your body ready.' We want to incorporate a very conscious inhale and exhale into the fun activities too.

30 seconds to experience it

Try changing your breathing pattern. For a few seconds take irregular breaths in and out that are deep and then shallow. Think of a crying child and how they breathe; try that pattern. How does it make you feel? Does it increase your stress level a little? Now, take a deep breath in, hold it for a second or two and slowly exhale. Do this a few times. How does this make your body feel?

Heavy muscle work

The proprioceptive system can help us feel organised, regulated and calm. Using your body is free, easy and always available. Heavy muscle work is any activity that engages your muscles or gives compression or traction through your joints. It is a fantastic tool for those moments when you are feeling overloaded and need to unload some sensory input. It can also wake you up and alert you when you are feeling shut down. Here are a few ways you can use your body:

Weight bearing (compression) through your joints: handstands, wheelbarrow walking, pushing yourself up on your hands while sitting on a chair (chair pushes), trying to push the wall over, lying over a therapy ball and propping yourself up with your arms, push-ups, jumping on a trampoline, running, jumping up and down.

Traction through the joints: throwing a ball, hanging from monkey bars or a pull-up bar on the door, hoovering, rock or tree climbing.

Heavy work such as carrying a washing basket or heavy backpack, household chores, gardening, kneading dough, swimming, building a den in the forest using heavy logs, pushing and pulling anything heavy, crawling up and down the stairs.

30 seconds to experience it

Put your hands in front of you in the prayer position and push them together as hard as you can for ten counts. Now hook your fingers together and pull apart as hard as you can without letting your hands come apart for ten counts. Shake out your hands. How does this make you feel? Does your body feel a tiny little more relaxed or focused?

Movement

The vestibular system is the first sensory system to develop in utero and is used from birth to help a baby calm. We rock a crying baby to soothe them or take them for a walk or drive when we need them to fall asleep. Movement is both calming and alerting. We must always use movement carefully though as it can easily overstimulate us and cause us to feel unwell. Never force a child to use a swing or to spin around. Remember, if it isn't fun then stop.

Movement can be up/down, front/back and circular/spinning (spinning can overstimulate people quickly so try to keep this to a minimum unless an occupational therapist has advised you).

Rocking slowly is calming and regulating and can be done on a park swing. Swing your child side to side in a sheet or towel, or try a rocking chair or rock with them on your lap or gently back and forth in a buggy.

Up/down movement can include jumping off logs in the park, jumping on a trampoline, jumping up the stairs one at a time and down again, jumping off the sofa onto cushions, sitting and bouncing on a therapy ball.

Spinning activities include holding their hands and spinning them around, or going on a playground roundabout. Encourage them to spin themselves, for example on an office chair.

You can also try running around the garden or park, cycling, scooter boards, roller blades or skate boards, going for a drive in the car.

30 seconds to experience it

Sitting where you are, shake your head vigorously side to side (be careful not to hurt your neck). If this is too much, then hang your head down between your knees. How does this make you feel? Nauseous? More awake? Unsettled? Calmer?

Touch

Deep pressure touch is a wonderful tool for calming a nervous system. There is a reason the market for beauty therapists to give massages is huge – we know it is good for us!

Deep pressure overrides light touch so is a fantastic way to help a child who is overwhelmed by tactile input. Give their feet a few squeezes before those dreaded socks go on and they may tolerate the socks. Deep pressure is as simple as it sounds. You can give a massage, deep hugs, wrap them in a blanket like a burrito and squeeze, lie them under two pillows and make a sandwich out of them, use a weighted blanket or a lap tray, pull all the cushions off the sofa and let them lie under those, roll a therapy ball up and down their body, give hand hugs (keep your hands flat and apply pressure through the limbs evenly).

Tactile play for your touch-seeking kids can include shaving foam, messy play with food, playdoh, different fabric textures, aqua beads, hide marbles or small toys in rice or pasta boxes, water play, mud play in the garden, searching for different texture leaves when out for a walk, picking up sticks, stones, conkers or prickly leaves when out and making a collection, sand play.

30 seconds to experience it

Gently squeeze your left arm with your right hand from your shoulder down to your wrist. Do the same with your right arm. Do you like the way it feels? Can you feel your body craving something more or is that enough for you? Reflect on how you like to be touched: light touch or deep, hard hugs?

Nature

The research to link nature with our mental and physical health is vast. We can unequivocally say that nature is good for us. It relieves stress, feeds our creativity and so much more. An exciting new therapy has emerged in the UK in recent years called ecosensory therapy (Slavin *et al.* 2022). Developed by occupational therapists Chris West and Clair Pemrick with their colleague, psychologist Dr Matt Slavin, this therapeutic intervention takes you out into nature. Here they have discovered we are often more able to regulate and connect with other humans, no matter what is going on inside our minds and bodies. Some of us have neglected our need for nature and become used to sitting indoors, using our screens to entertain us.

Local parks or even a garden can provide so many opportunities for you and your child. Sometimes it is too hard to go to the park or find an open space. You don't need to go to a nature reserve to discover the power of nature. Walking to school can be a moment to use nature by taking notice of the trees or how the clouds are moving in the sky, collecting a few stones or twigs or listening to the sound of the birds. Building dens out of logs, playing in the mud, balancing on logs, climbing trees, jumping from one stone to another, using a hammock outside or simply taking a snack and eating it on the grass instead of in the house are all simple, free ways to regulate outside.

30 seconds to experience it

Are you inside at the moment? What can you hear? A clock ticking, the TV in the background, the sound of somebody talking on the phone? What does the air feel like to breathe? Now step outside, into the garden or onto the balcony or simply open a window and lean out a tiny bit. How does the air feel to breathe now? What can you hear? Birds, airplane in the sky, perhaps a bee buzzing if it is the summer? Do you feel any different inside versus outside?

Music

Debs Dana (2018) tells us that music can modulate and activate the brain. It has the unique ability to create connection between human beings by increasing trust and empathy. Music can activate the social engagement system and bring us out of fight, flight or freeze. Debs Dana advocates the use of music within therapy sessions. Many of us will relate to the way music can change our mood, lift us up on a darker day or quieten our mind on an anxious day. Music can be used in so many ways and with all our technology, we have access to nearly every type of musical genre known to man.

Create a playlist with your child, and for yourself with songs to calm their bodies down, wake them up, help them focus or fill them with joy. Use music as a timer; for example, challenge them to get dressed before their favourite song is done or to brush their teeth while a funny song is playing. When they need a good, intense movement break, play a song and dance around the room, encouraging them to move as much as possible. Join them for the dance – you will be surprised at how much better you feel afterwards. Music is a powerful sensory tool.

30 seconds to experience it

Find your favourite song on your chosen platform. As it plays, take note of how it makes you feel. Do you have a memory that comes up? Does the song fill you with peace or cause you to tap your foot? Do you feel any different after you have listened to it?

Auditory

Some of our sensory kids can get quickly overwhelmed by loud or noisy places. Loud unexpected sounds like a hand dryer or a siren can push them into fight, flight or freeze instantly. If your child struggles with this, I would strongly recommend you consult with an occupational therapist. There are some wonderful therapeutic interventions that might help your child's auditory system manage loud noise more easily. The use of ear defenders and noise-reducing ear plugs can help when you know you cannot avoid a noisy space. Remember to get advice about how long to use these for as each of us is unique.

30 seconds to reflect

How much noise can you tolerate before you need things to be quiet? Do you need the radio off in the car when you are driving somewhere new or can you focus with the music playing? Can you read this book with the TV sound on or do you need quiet to concentrate?

Useful equipment

★ Body sock (can also be used for tug of war or to pull along on a scooter board)
★ Weighted products, for example weighted toys, lap blanket
★ Lycra tunnel
★ Therapy ball or peanut ball – can be used as a seat at the table or to watch TV, for gaming or for squashing or muscle-strengthening games
★ Resistance bands

- ★ Pop up tent with simple lights, cushions, lava lamp (if safe)
- ★ Scooter board
- ★ Crash mat (you could make one by filling a duvet cover with old pillows or blankets so it is thick and soft)
- ★ Trampoline or trampette
- ★ Gorilla gym
- ★ Pull up bar for the door
- ★ Theraputty

Pound shop items

- ★ Straws (for games that help regulate)
- ★ Bubbles
- ★ Hand cream (for massage)
- ★ Playdoh or Blu Tack
- ★ Fidget toys
- ★ Resistance band (for example, around the chair legs)
- ★ Glitter jar/liquid timers
- ★ Marbles

Conclusion

Here we are, at the end of our journey together. We may not have found the 'magic wand solution' that can instantly help your child regulate, but we have discovered strategies that are more powerful than we may have realised. In a cheesy but relevant metaphor, some of what we have discussed is a little like a small stone being tossed onto water. The stone can be tiny yet cause ripples that move further than expected. The tiny stone even changes the way the water moves beneath the surface where you can't always see clearly. Small, consistent changes in ourselves can be that powerful too.

Our own stories matter – where we come from and the kind of parenting we have been raised with matter. All through my parenting journey, my mother, who passed away before my girls were even born, has tagged along. The legacy of how her mother parented her laid the foundations for how she raised me, my sister and my brother. The home my grandmother created for her, filled with abuse and addiction, was handed to my mother. She did the very best she could with her genetics and environment and broke the cycle of addiction and abuse, but in the end she had no choice but to hand some of her brokenness on to me. I am a healthier version of my mother yet still often felt that I had little choice in how I reacted to my sensory child. Changing the dance my child and I were in had to start with me. Learning a new way of reacting to her sensory needs and meltdowns was eye-opening. Small little changes in me had big effects on how she managed her overwhelming sensory needs. I know this can be true for us all.

We have said it many times throughout this book: there are as many ways to parent as there are humans on the earth. Nobody can write a book that reflects all parts of our unique lives and personalities, but some facts are fundamentally true for all humans. They are what we have explored throughout the book.

We began with learning more about what the sensory systems are and how they change the way we perceive the world, not just for our sensory children but also for ourselves. The window of tolerance and what fight, flight and freeze do to our brains helped us reflect on what might be the underlying cause of the behaviours we see in ourselves and our children. This deeper understanding began to give us the knowledge we need to have more compassion for our children and possibly even for ourselves as we navigate parenting a sensory child.

The animal analogies have provided a language and platform for us to reflect on how we react to the sensory needs and meltdowns we experience with our children. The jellyfish is highly attuned to the emotions of others but can be easily wobbled by them; the rhino is fiercely loyal and protective but can tend to control situations; the kangaroo is nurturing and provides for our children's needs extraordinarily well but can be overprotective; the ostrich cares deeply for the family and looks after them well but can show too little emotion. The dolphin and St Bernard give us some ideas for connection, looking after ourselves, setting boundaries, having fun with our children and celebrating the moments we do well.

We ended with sensory strategies that we can use when planning how to manage our trickier moments. We have given ourselves permission to fail at times; we can't be perfect parents.

This is the start of something great for you and for your family. I can say with confidence that you can change how your child will live their life as they grow up and how they parent if they have a family of their own one day. A healthier, more reflective parent raises a healthier, more able child. This is my hope for you, that you notice how much power you have to change the present and the future. Search for others who understand and can support you, because parenting a sensory child can easily be lonely and hard. There are so many of us that want to be part of your journey, and that is why so many charities and online platforms exist – parents who want to walk alongside you and strengthen you when you need it. Educate those friends and family who are willing; give them opportunities to help you. Be kind to yourself and celebrate what you are already doing well.

Don't put this book away just yet; keep it close to hand and refer back to the pages that spoke to you. Mark the pages, underline the sentences. Parenting is not a sprint, it is a marathon. We have to look after ourselves, equip ourselves as our children grow and change, but most of all, we can dust ourselves off and start again when we fall. You have got this!

References

Aschbacherab, K., O'Donovan, A., Wolkowitz, O.M. & Dhabhar, F.S. (2013). Good stress, bad stress and oxidative stress: Insights from anticipatory cortisol reactivity. *Psychoneuroendocrinology*, 38(9), 1698–1708.

Bundy, A.C., Lane, S.J. & Murray, E.A. (2002). *Sensory Integration Theory and Practice*. Philadelphia, PA: F.A. Davis Company.

Christakis, N. & Fowler, J. (2011). *Connected: The Amazing Power of Social Networks and How They Shape Our Lives*. London: HarperPress.

Coan, J.A. & Sbarra, D.A. (2015). Social baseline theory: The social regulation of risk and effort. *Current Opinion in Psychology*, 1, 87–91.

Dana, D. (2018). *The Polyvagal Theory in Therapy*. New York, NY: W.W. Norton & Company.

Dana, D. (2019, December 5). Story Follows State – Investigating Polyvagal Theory. (S. Marriott & A. Kelly, interviewers)

Dell'Amore, C. (2013, July 23). Dolphins have 'names,' respond when called. *National Geographic*. Retrieved from www.nationalgeographic.com/animals/article/130722-dolphins-whistle-names-identity-animals-science.

Dunn, W. (1997). The impact of sensory processing abilities on the daily lives of young children and their families: A conceptual model. *Infants & Young Children*, 9(4), 23–35.

Dunn, W. (2008). *Living Sensationally*. London: Jessica Kingsley Publishers.

Kas, D. (2019, April 26). The St Bernard: The making of an Alpine legend. *House of Switzerland*. Retrieved from www.houseofswitzerland.org/swissstories/history/st-bernard-making-alpine-legend.

Koscinski, C.N. (2018). *Interoception: How I Feel*. London: Martin Publishing Services.

Kranowitz, C.S. (2005). *The Out-of-Sync Child*. New York, NY: Penguin Random House.

Metz, A.E. & Bolin, D. (2019). Dunn's Model of Sensory Processing: An investigation of the axes of the four-quadrant model in healthy adults. *Brain Sciences*, 9(2), 35.

Payne, K.J. (2019). *Being at Your Best When Your Kids Are at Their Worst*. Boulder, CO: Shambhala Publications.

Porges, S. (2011). *The Polyvagal Theory: Neurophysiological Foundations of Emotions, Attachment, Communication, and Self-regulation*. New York, NY: W.W. Norton & Company.

Rheem, D. (2018, November 13). *Don Rheem*. Retrieved from https://donrheem. com/social-baseline-theory-at-work.

Siegel, D.J. (2020). *The Developing Mind* (third edition). New York, NY: Guilford Press.

Siegel, D.J. & Bryson, T.P. (2011). *The Whole-Brain Child*. London: Robinson.

Slavin, M., Pemrick, C. & West, C. (2022). *Ecosensory Therapy*. Retrieved from www.ecosensorytherapy.com/research.

Taylor, J. (2016, July 25). *Mirror neurons after a quarter century: New light, new cracks*. Harvard University. Retrieved from https://sitn.hms.harvard.edu/ flash/2016/mirror-neurons-quarter-century-new-light-new-cracks.

Treasure, J., Smith, G. & Crane, A. (2007). *Skills-based Learning for Caring for a Loved One with an Eating Disorder*. London: Routledge.

Tronick, D.E. (2007). Still Face Experiment. YouTube. Retrieved from https:// thepowerofdiscord.com.

Twohig-Bennett, C. & Jones, A. (2018). The health benefits of the great out-doors: A systematic review and meta-analysis of greenspace exposure and health outcomes. *Environmental Research*, 166, 628–637.

Index